JWJ

(Journey with Jesus)

WENDY GILL ROCCO

ISBN 979-8-88751-932-6 (paperback)
ISBN 979-8-88751-933-3 (digital)

Christian Faith Publishing
832 Park Avenue
Meadville, PA 16335
www.christianfaithpublishing.com

Printed in the United States of America

I dedicate this book to my friend Kay, whose personal Journey with Jesus began five days before she entered paradise.

Opening Message from the Author

✦

As humans, we must live the life we were created for—and we all have the power to make a difference in this world right where we are, with Jesus at the helm. In my world, this book is twenty-five years in the making and is most definitely a vision given to me from God. You might ask, so after that long, what has gotten me to this point to completion? As the Bible shares, he who began a good work in you will be faithful to complete it, and He most certainly created a path and the timing for His glory, as since my original vision, He has allowed us all to experience other compelling stories to share with you that demonstrate his mercy and faithfulness. **PRAISE REPORT!**

The positioning of *JWJ* centers around how, after surviving multiple years of uncertainty as a world, we are all reprioritizing what is important to us—thinking of our life's Journey overall as an ongoing adventure with a purpose.

Since I started writing many years ago, my overlying inspiration of this part of my Journey has been the Bible verse Romans 8:28: "And we know that all things work together for good to them that love God, to them who are the called according to his purpose." You will read about amazing things that God has done both in my life as well as many others to not only provide and sustain us but to BLESS us in good and seemingly bad times. Yes, this book has an emphasis on the bad times because we all go through them. And when we do, we typically get side-blinded by being in the moment and forget to look for the light at the end of the tunnel. And that's an amazingly hard place to be… BUT THERE IS ALWAYS LIGHT. Let's prepare for all things unknown by staying positive *now* and allowing God to intervene and support the *then*. Yes, expect the good, but prepare for the worst; it's a part of all of our lives. Just by recognizing this upfront and not being surprised when it happens, you will stand firmer in allowing God to lead you through it. Your relationship with God can make it a very different experience because the truth is, we don't always know the beauty that can result from difficult and seemingly bad situations—BUT GOD DOES!

God has made beautiful things come from seemingly bad situations. Read on and be inspired,* and more importantly, let this equip you to face life's challenges with joy in knowing that God has a better plan for your life. Everyone is given different challenges, some based on the choices we've faced and decisions we have made. Find true purpose and build a legacy in your personal Journey with the Living God!

*In true Wendy fashion, I will reference God-influenced inspiration throughout this book as a **PRAISE REPORT!** But you will certainly recognize them on your own.

Introduction

✦

Jesus came so you might enjoy *your* life most abundantly (John 10:10).

This book is about enjoying and appreciating every day of your life even in seemingly bad times or through instances of bad experiences. To provide insight about the author, please know that I am a regular person, with issues, problems, and shortcomings as we all do. Let's face it, and please don't be fooled—NOBODY is perfect.

Living our lives with a personal relationship with Jesus does not exempt us from hard times or from being tempted to do things we know we should not. We are all going to experience these instances throughout our lifetime. As my son recently reminded me, it is so important to recognize that even Jesus himself, GOD MADE FLESH, did not experience a perfect, problem-free life on earth— He was put down, bullied, belittled, not trusted, accused of being self-righteous, and ultimately, murdered, hung on a cross in front of the whole community. Why would we expect anything less? The truth is, we grow through pain, and without it, we would not appreciate all the GOOD in our lives!

> Dear friends, do not be surprised at the
> fiery ordeal that has come on you to test you,
> as though something strange were happening to
> you. (1 Peter 4:12)

I am writing this book to share not only personal details of my life's Journey by describing the way God has become a ROCK for me in the not-so-good times but of others as well who have shared their intimate stories (Psalm 95). We are all sharing the tapestry of thread throughout our lives to show God's love, protection, and provision by sharing what God can and will provide in a time of trouble to confirm our path to hopefulness. We only need to ask. In Exodus 32:11–14, the Bible shares that we don't' have because we don't ask. We will learn to ask in His name and His will. This asking is also known as prayer, but it's more than that. It's a relationship with your Creator. It only makes sense that prayer is a conversation with the Lord, not a repetitious poem as mentioned in Matthew 6:7.

Throughout my life I have been collecting small rocks—not just any rock, but rocks that I see in interesting places and times that just happen to be shaped like a heart. I call them my Heart Rock Collection, and I have them placed around my home in strategic places as well as some collectively in a few glass bowls, as they remind me of all the love and happy memories over the years that I have been blessed to experience. And yes, I am grateful to still be able to collect them!

It's true and no secret that we all take a different path in this one life that God has given us. What we do with this life is the product of our own free will and a result of our personal choices. I am encouraging you to choose to make your life a deliberate, positive, impactful one. Sure, this includes taking care of yourself—eating well, being as physically fit as viable, supplementing your vitamin needs, drinking water, all the things we have learned and know that we need to do to take care of the one body we have been given genetically to the best of our ability in hopes that these actions will extend the Journey and, ultimately, our impact in this world. That is our own responsibility. I also understand based on my own personal health challenges that these things do not necessarily guarantee anything, and it's ultimately in God's hands and for His purpose, if you allow it to be.

What about our spiritual body? How are we nurturing that?

This brings us to FREE will. What does this mean to you? Does it mean you can do whatever you want? Actually, it does, but it also means we can do what we choose to be closer to our Creator. This is how we nurture our spiritual needs.

Early in my professional career, I had an opportunity to work with a project mentor. I will refer to him as Jay. Jay was a bright man in his thirties. He had a family, was an avid cycler, worked out regularly, and appeared to be in great health. He was a huge influencer to me in my early procurement training, and I learned to greatly appreciate him.

After several months of project work, my team and I were on a weekly call, but he was not on the call, and that was not like him. Later that day, we all learned that he had suffered from a sudden heart attack. It just seemed unreal. While traveling out of state to see another client, he was working out in the hotel gym and just passed away. This was devastating news and shook up the entire team as you could imagine. We were shocked and hurting, and for some time, we experienced a void in our lives. I can only imagine the pain and shock his family suffered as well.

I share this message because we all know or have personally experienced stories like this one, when our family or friends are impacted because as much as we can try and plan, life is not predictable, nor is it promised to us. It is reality that nothing in this life is guaranteed, but it is the precise reason we need to have a personal relationship with God, our Creator and true stable life companion. So ultimately, until our own life ends (and this will happen, my friend, because no one will live on this earth forever, and we will all one day meet our Maker), we can live this one lifetime with the confidence in knowing that God "has our back" until this life on earth has been completed to His will.

In a deeper sense, we all desire to experience faith, hope, and love while we are on this earth. God has brought me to this point in pouring out my heart and life experiences to comfort, encourage, and bring hope to purposely inspire you to make your Journey more positive, powerful, and exciting, and to live your BEST LIFE, feel valued, and at the same time build a legacy of your own to help and support others.

The Bible tells us in the book of 1 John 5:14–15 to have confidence in approaching God, that if we ask anything according to His will, He hears us. And if we know that he hears us, whatever we ask, we know that we have what we asked of him. Sharing our stories is powerful, so please make it a point to share how God has answered your prayers and be a blessing to others.

In sharing examples of God's incredible mercies, we can help each other experience comfort, encouragement, and healing—and NOW IS CERTAINLY THE TIME. We are all on a Journey; the only difference is in the route we choose to take. I encourage you to take the road that begins with Jesus and leads to everlasting life.

As Mother Teresa once shared, she didn't look for Jesus in herself; she saw Jesus's face in everyone she looked upon. If you do not know Jesus as your personal Lord and Savior at this point in your life, please read on and experience for yourself the powerful impact He has made in the lives of so many who have chosen to share their stories and experiences. Then consider for yourself—could you spend the rest of your God-given days making a positive impact on others along the way?

In the final pages of this book, you will better understand how to take more conscientious steps of asking Jesus into your heart as a sojourner so you too can begin the most incredible Journey of your lifetime, no matter what age or stage of life you are in. What is your legacy? My prayer is that you have the courage to say YES to the gift that He has in store for you because you are His child. But it is ultimately your choice.

If you do not experience a daily walk with Jesus, you may need to ask Him into your heart, or maybe you have, but you just haven't spent time with Him lately nurturing the relationship. Please take time today to recommit yourself to Him and begin again to allow His power to flow through you. Imagine that you too can be a vessel for the Almighty God!

Some people I have met along the way remember the exact moment they accepted Jesus into their hearts and lives; others have no clue. They have done it too many times to confirm or to reaffirm the connection. I am in the latter group, and I am not discouraged by this because I now know the true joy is in the Journey itself.

In sharing my Journey and the amazing ways our Maker and my companion has been there for me, my hope is to encourage you on your Journey. Read on, sojourner. The stories you are about to read are true and reflect many life experiences that God has blessed us with by allowing our paths to cross along the way. Know that the important thing is not so much when your Journey begins, and it's never too late, but that at some point, it does and then continues to mature throughout your life. The *J* in our *Journey* represents Jesus Christ, our Lord and Savior. John 3:16 (NKJ) says: "For God so loved the world that he gave his only begotten son, that whomever believes in him shall not perish, but have eternal life." Once this critical decision is made, YOUR JOYFUL JOURNEY begins.

Chapter J = Jesus Brings Joy to the Journey

✦

Achieving real JOY begins with putting **J**esus first, **O**thers second, and **Y**ourself last. These words of wisdom were shared with me by my then eight-year-old son—*truly from the mouths of babes.*

But the real question is, do you really know Jesus, or do you just know of Him?

As I recall upon my high school graduation, it was a hot June afternoon. I was wearing a bright-pink sundress that I had purchased at a thrift store for the occasion. I don't remember much else because I was so consumed with looking for my parents in the audience that nothing else seemed to matter at that moment. It was a large crowd, and I did not connect with them, and I went back to my sister's house with my diploma in hand. This was a serious accomplishment for me considering the last four months of my senior year were spent living wherever I could find a place to stay.

You see, my parents were amazing people. They loved me, and although through meager means, they demonstrated that love by making sure I had a quality education. They sacrificed to send me to private schools, and ultimately, I graduated from North Catholic High School. Even with this love and giving spirit, I was a difficult teenager to live with, and being the fourth child and quite the rebel, I was allowed to move out. I felt I was sparing them from the aggravation of raising another messed-up teen. Yes, we all had our issues in life to contend with—results of our own choices. And as I have learned over the years, being a parent is probably the toughest thing you can experience. As I share with my loved ones, it's the hardest *job* you will ever *love*. The Bible addresses this relationship as well in not just one area of the Bible because of its importance: "Love and honor your parents" (mother and father). And it offers us a promise: "So that it may go well with you, and that you may enjoy a long life on earth" (Ephesians 6:2–3).

Below is a picture of my tribute to my parents that I created and gave to them as a gift quite a few years back, and they still have it displayed, so I know it was as meaningful to them as it was for me. Take time to thank your parents for their love and sacrifice—somehow, someway!

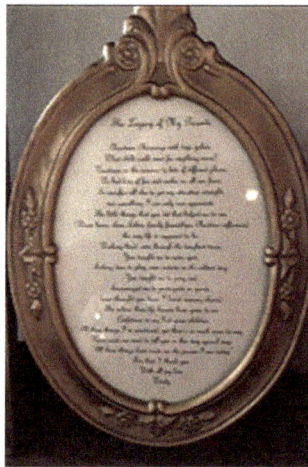

Although my teen years were rough, I survived. I use the word *survived* literally. I had experienced devastating events and had to make overwhelming decisions that shaped my life forever. My first decision was to wait on getting a college degree because I had to work to make a living for myself. Secondly, I was planning on getting married to an emotionally and physically abusive boyfriend, my first true love, or at least what I perceived as love at that time. He was very popular in our circle, so infatuation maybe? I thought that he would change, and in retrospect, don't we all? LOL. However, even during my pregnancy with our child, he was just as abusive, if not more. I feared for my life on occasion.

I attribute much of his abuse to drugs and alcohol, and it finally caught up with us. Soon after our son was born, I ended up in the hospital with a broken nose and fractured hand as a result of one of his furies. My mother was in such fear for my life that she was putting an insurance policy on it if I was to go back with him because she just knew he was going to kill me in one of these times of rage. I decided to take her advice and seek counseling. After committing to a one-hour session with the psychiatrist, I knew I needed to protect myself and, more importantly, my son. I also realized that I was probably in need of ongoing counseling for my mental health. The fact that I would put up with a person treating me like that surely demonstrated that I must have had some deep-rooted issues of my own to work out. I now realize that I was insecure and suffered from an extremely low self-esteem, and at times, I did not value my own life. Fortunately, I have come a long way removed from those days. **PRAISE REPORT!**

The first thing that majorly opened my eyes was my college experience. I attended the local community college for four years (we called it the Northside University, but it is typically a two-year experience). In that time frame, I began to live a changed lifestyle. I started to become the party animal type because I felt I missed that in my youth by being a young mother. I began drinking on the weekends and partying with my friends when I had a break and a babysitter. And I moved residences a lot to several different neighborhoods during those years, but I never did move out of Pittsburgh. The life of a renter, I guess. At times I had to rely on welfare for supplemental financial support while I attended school. This was definitely a humiliation that drove me to being self-sufficient. I hated the negative self-inflicted feelings I got while standing in line to get my welfare check and the dreaded food stamps, but I needed them to feed my son. And yes, at that time, you had to stand in line. I also worked a part-time deli job between classes where I made meal deliveries for the lunch-hour rush to several businesses, engaging specifically with business professionals, and I just knew someday I would be one of them. (And for the last twenty-five-plus years I have, with all praise and glory to God.) **PRAISE REPORT!**

During that time of my life, I met a nice guy who was a real gentleman. He was someone who treated me with more respect than anyone had ever done in my entire life, and for that he was not just anyone. He personally demonstrated self-respect, a great self-esteem, and held a terrific job to support his family. I respected him for those things. I saw in him the things that I wanted to possess in my own life. At the time we met, he was separated from his wife, and I was single; so we dated a few times, and I fell in love with him but all the time never feeling his equal.

Right around that same time, I had a traumatic life experience where there was a murder attempt on my life. It was an off-the-wall, freaky situation that happened with my life insurance agent. It turned out that I reminded him of a woman he had a child with, but he was cut off from them. With that, he flipped out one night, apparently high on drugs, and started calling me, saying weird things, although at this point, I did not know it was him on the call. I immediately called the police station to report the threats, but they stated that 99.9 percent of these types of calls turn out to be nothing. Taking that advice into consideration, I just stopped answering the phone. Remember, this was a time when we did not have cell phones, and we didn't know who or where these incoming calls were from.

I put my son in his crib, fed Buddy (my friend's pit bull that I was dog-sitting at the time) and then lay down on the couch to watch a TV show. Then it happened. I heard weird noises outside the house, and when I looked out, I saw a not-so-familiar car parked there. Immediately after, I heard a strange knock on my apartment door, like a *ching-ching*, not a *knock-knock*. When I asked who was there, I heard his voice, and he was telling me he wanted to come in so he could get my insurance premium payment. Now, that was just too weird. It was very late in the evening, and that was not appropriate. This was the insurance man that my in-laws had connected me with earlier in the year. He seemed like a decent guy, but this was completely inappropriate. At this point, the dog was reacting strangely and barking crazily. All I could think was that I really didn't want him to wake up my sleeping baby. Things then got quiet, and I assumed he was leaving. I never made the connection with the strange calls and now this. And when I looked outside the window from my second-floor apartment to confirm he had left by watching him drive away, he didn't. Instead, he reached in his car and pulled out a sawed-off shotgun and began handling it like he was loading it. I totally freaked out!

I immediately called 911, shared what was happening, cried with fear, and instinctively went to the furthest point of the apartment to divert anything away from where my son was sleeping in the bedroom. This was the kitchen, so I kept hold of the phone and cord and told the 911 agent to tell my family I loved them, as I honestly believed he was going to kill me that night. I stayed with her on the call as I pulled the phone around the apartment with me in panic.

As I saw him enter the apartment building, I climbed outside the kitchen window on a small porch eaves, and within minutes, which felt like hours, the police showed up. I heard yelling and scuffling inside the hallway from where I was "hiding" on the eaves, and finally the 911 agent reassured me that it was safe to go back into the house as they had the perpetrator in custody. It was just too crazy. I was frozen out there—not temperature frozen, but mentally and physically frozen. The officers helped me get back into the house where I immediately then checked on my son. I shared everything I could with the officer and then called a good friend to come get us. I had to get out of that apartment.

Interestingly enough, I escaped the crazy, intoxicated husband from killing me and then to experience this…it was way too much for a young woman out on her own with a young child to have to go through. I thought I was tough, but this shook my world. It turned out that I reminded him of the mother of his child, and she was not letting him see him, so he seemingly wanted to take it out on me. I did get some help through this, but it would later rear its ugly head back up at me in the form of a post-traumatic stress disorder (PTSD). More to come on this. The good news was, God had my back, and this out-of-control man did not kill me that crazy night. Sure, I was a bit messed up socially, mentally, and other ways because of that experience, but ultimately, my son and I survived. **PRAISE REPORT!**

I did reach out to my new friend, later to become the love of my life, and he was there to support and help me through that tough time. But soon after, he did share with me that he was going to try to get back with his estranged wife in an attempt of making his failing marriage work because it was important to him to be there for his children. He ended up moving three hundred miles across the state to Harrisburg. I truly wanted him to be happy, so I said goodbye and wished him all the best. I also began to pray for him, that his marriage would work out, as I knew firsthand how hard it was to be a single parent.

It was then that I began attending a neighborhood church. My only son at that time was attending their childcare program, and they offered a significant discount if you attended their Sunday service. Of course, I would take advantage of the discount (That's just how God made me, and if you know me, you know it's true!), but what I found there was yet another interesting experience in my life. I met an older man, a so-called elder in that church, who was teaching me about the Bible. He was a bit older than I was, and I was not attracted to him at all—physically or otherwise. I just appreciated that he could answer my questions about God and the Bible.

See, at this time of my life, I was under the care of a psychiatrist due to PTSD as a result of the murder attempt and was visiting my estranged husband at a maximum-security prison "so our son would know his daddy"…the man who went crazy one night, all buzzed up on drugs, stole his father's handgun, and robbed several north side businesses until chased, shot, and then caught by the police, therefore, earning the title "The North Side Bandit." Now this is where my life was—I was in love with a married man and married to the North Side Bandit, but I was wholeheartedly seeking a better life. I began learning about how God loves me just the way I am and right where I was at that time. I really saw something to this God stuff, especially because I was introduced to God on several occasions throughout my life in my past. I wanted to get something from it all right, the three things I lacked and had wanted to possess for so long: respect, self-esteem, and security.

And now, looking back, I know God's hand was in my life throughout, since as a child I accepted Jesus at an altar at the Assembly of God in Allison Park with my entire immediate family—yes, more to come on this story as well.

Feeling so desperate at this time, I accepted Jesus into my heart once again, and amazingly my life changed, like three hundred and sixty degrees, probably too fast as you will see, but good things primarily resulted. I stopped entertaining the party life and quit drinking. Those party-like relationships were no longer appealing to me anymore. While visiting my now-ex-husband one afternoon, I felt like God was telling me to wait for him, that he would come to know Jesus too and turn his life around. Not that this was something I personally wanted to do because of major trust issues (as you can imagine). It actually scared me to have these thoughts because this was the same man who abused me and almost choked me to death on one occasion. But I believed that all things are possible with God as the center and in control.

As I shared these feelings with my new "biblical advisor," he seemed extremely against this idea. He said that I should not think like that. He then told me that God was telling him that he and I should be married, but honestly, that seemed to be even stranger to me. God did not tell me to go there, and furthermore, I shared that I did not have romantic feelings for him. He kept using God in his defense at my questions concerning this issue.

At this point, I was a newly life-changed Christian, but still an adult with a lot of past baggage and devastating past experiences. In fact, my psychiatrist advised me firmly to not make any life-changing decisions for at least a year from my PTSD-causing experience. But I struggled with all of this input because I wanted to do God's will in my life and wasn't sure what that entailed. (WARNING: If it's from God, you will know it in your heart.)

Looking back, I am fully convinced that this was a form of spiritual, emotional, and/or religious abuse, and here's why. I was "manipulated" into thinking that this meant I was to marry this guy, or I may never experience the three characteristics I longed for. So after knowing him for a total of eight months, we were married even though this was against the better judgment of all my genuine friends and family. They were convinced that I was brainwashed into marrying him. And it turns out, I should have listened to their advice because I realized on the night of the wedding that I made a huge mistake, at that time thinking maybe one of the biggest of my life. I tried to be intimate but found myself having to force the situation—not good. I couldn't stop thinking of the man I had fallen genuinely in love with. The gentleman who possessed what I truly longed for in myself. The man who made me a better person just by being around him. Yes, the man living three hundred miles away with his wife and two young kids. How pathetic was I?

When we returned from the honeymoon, the marriage was definitely over. I told him I did not love him. God did not give me those feelings for stepping out in faith as he described He would. I was certain that I had made a terrible decision and seriously wanted a divorce.

Three weeks later, I realized I had become pregnant from that encounter. In my mind, I thought this could only happen to me. I spent the next eight months making arrangements to give this child up for adoption to a Christian couple who would be able to care for this child in a way I felt I could not. It was one of the most difficult decisions I had ever had to make, but being a struggling single mother already, I was convinced it was the right thing to do for my unborn child first and foremost. His future life experience was at risk and far too critical.

Later in my pregnancy, my mother made me vow that I would keep him if the baby was not born perfect. Since I had just had a sonogram, and the baby was described as perfect, I knew I could keep the promise. But God had another plan. He must have wanted me to be the mother of this child because he was in fact born with a problem that made him sickly. He had a rare late gestational diaphragmatic hernia and needed medical and surgical attention immediately after birth to repair the diaphragm and pull down the smothered organs. I couldn't believe my ears when the doctor confronted me with this news. How could this have happened? I was certain by the sonogram result that this baby was perfect. Yes, God had another plan.

After the surgery and many days later, I chose to keep the promise to my mother and raise my son on my own. I know I must have hurt others with my decision, and believe me, I was quite scared myself. I now can so clearly see how God used these circumstances and this child to make me a better mother and to bring me closer to God. He provided for my baby in ways I could have never guessed possible.

In fact, I was living in an unfurnished and uncarpeted home at the time, and there was no clothing for the baby since I wasn't expecting to bring him home, but God provided and met our needs. My ex-in-laws just happened at that time to move into a furnished home and gave me all of their previous furnishings. I was approved on a loan from Sears to get a carpeting loan, but I didn't have any credit or a full-time job, so I know that was a miracle. My first child's yia yia was amazingly giving and caring, and she purchased an abundance of new clothing to welcome this child home. They knew we were in need, and so did God. He touched their hearts to make that all happen, and today I'm so much closer to God because I have seen His hand directly moved to change our circumstances, to help change our lives in a positive light. So when you feel God prompting you to help provide or support something He puts on your heart, ACT on it and BE the blessing!

Due to his hernia birth situation, he was asthmatic for the first two years of his life and required daily breathing treatments, and being his primary caretaker as well as financial and emotional support… This was where I began to learn what I was made of because I was forced to handle even more responsibilities on my own, but more importantly, I was greatly aware of all the support God was providing me.

All things are possible through Christ who
strengthens me. (Philippians 4:13)

That is exactly why we must hold close to and lean on our faith in those times when we can't understand what, how, or why God has allowed something seemingly negative to come into our lives. We need only to keep ourselves available in humility. Stay hopeful; there is always a blessing on its way. And stay confident on the promises of God and recall Romans 8:28 from which this book is grounded, where the key part of that verse is "for those who love the lord, and are called according to his purpose." We are ALL called according to His purpose.

Growing in faith is a lifelong Journey. As God slowly walks you through life with your hands tightly in His, you become more confident in Him, in His faithfulness. In good times and bad times, stay open to the possibilities because He always proves Himself faithful.

Also, during this time, I was able to again see the man I truly loved more because although he and his wife tried, they could not mend their relationship and separated once again, leading to a divorce. We reconnected, and he was there for me as a friend and supported and encouraged me along the way.

One thing led to another, and we began to have a romantic and more intimate relationship. And then my third pregnancy happened. I felt somewhat defeated, third child to third relationship, but knew I was a child of God, and I began to seek Him more closely and asked Him back into my life.

In retrospect, GOD never left me—He waited for me to lean on Him. The only difference was that this time, I wanted to know and do His will for my life. This time not for selfish reasons, and this had been a first for me when it came to my relationship with God. I truly wanted to be a servant. I was broken…and was going to get the perspective right this time, contrary to the time before when I made a mistake of marrying for reasons other than real, true love in my heart. And for that, I am just heartfully grateful that I didn't think it was too late for me to make things right.

Interestingly enough, this all drove me to pray a great deal about being in God's will. On January 7 of that year, I had my third son on his father's birthday. What are the odds? I still feel to this day that it was a sign from God letting me know He was with me through all of it.

A few months later, I managed to finish the credits required to attain my associates degree by the time my third son was six months old.

The trials of my life had begun to take me to the place I longed to be. The accomplishments of my life's Journey to this point with God's grace had helped me in this ongoing process. Everything was working together for the good like Romans 8:28 proclaims. The three things I respected so much in the man I fell in love with were beginning to manifest in my own life. I was beginning to respect this new person I was becoming. I found a new self-esteem that was stemming from my personal accomplishments and being responsible—selflessly. And although I did, however, choose at that time not to marry this man I loved because of the two failures in my past, I felt very much in God's will.

I was getting closer to God, day by day, by reading and trusting in His Word and being a servant in other areas by helping others in my sphere of influence. Loving Jesus for who He was and not for what He could do for me—this is where I found my security, not in myself or the man I loved, not in the church or its people, but in the ever-present loving arms of God. Once I reached this understanding, I knew it was okay to get married and probably the right thing to do to be an example for my young children.

On September 30, 1994, I married the love of my life. We share a mutual respect for each other, and together we experience the joys and pains of sharing each other's lives and some of the beautiful, and not-so-beautiful areas of our pasts. Today we are the textbook example of a blended family, and although I do not recommend this lifestyle to others because of the challenges it poses, trusting in God and allowing Him to be our focus is what keeps us straight. We are certainly an example that all things are possible with God and His love, forgiveness, and support.

That is where I am today. I believe I am living the Journey of my life that God has ordained for me based on my past choices— both good and bad. I try to approach life on a daily basis, knowing that each day is a gift. I pray for those I love and those my life touches and see it as God has allowed it. My sole purpose of writing my story is in hopes that the pains and struggles of my life's Journey can benefit another life. I know that God can use the traumatic events that both I and others have experienced in our lives for the benefit and inspiration of others.

As my Journey progressed, I was a young mother of three sons, had completed my associate's degree in nutrition management, and prayed to God for an actual vision to be able to provide for my family because I didn't want to rely on anyone other than myself to ultimately provide for my children. Yes, I was married at this point but still wanted to never take that for granted. Within weeks of prayer and conversations with God, I had visual direction to open a resale clothing store, not the uppity kind that was higher-end and higher-priced, but a clean and well-organized boutique that appealed to women seeking lower-cost options and still be fashionable wherever they were in life. See, I am an avid resale shopper, not only because I had limited funds during my Journey, but also because I am a huge advocate of recycling.

To best prepare myself for this next step in my life, I began meeting with a local college that offered a small business development center. There I learned from retired and once-successful business owners on how to write a business plan so I could seek out the funding for my start-up. It took several months to complete, but the time spent was surely well worth it.

Shortly after I completed my business plan, I was blessed once again. My now-husband (and love of my life) was working out of town at this time, and out of thin air, without any notice, he was offered a job with his company that required him to relocate to State College, or otherwise take a severance package. Since he so much desired to be close to all of his family, he took the severance and invested ten thousand dollars in my vision. **PRAISE REPORT!** God's timing is amazing, my friends!

I am happy to report that it was an investment well spent. I was able to find the right location and secure a fourteen hundred square foot storefront in a cultural district of Pittsburgh. (This location was also very much prayerfully decided upon.) This business venture not only allowed us to provide for the family; it was an amazing life Journey in itself. THE BIGGER GIFT: For the seven years invested, I learned hands-on about business, which ultimately propelled me later in life into a successful business career. I was able to unleash my innovative and creative side—like an MBA experience without the schoolbooks, paper degree, or COST (Yeah!). And what I still consider the best part of that experience was the amazing people I met. I am truly grateful for this experience and the lessons learned. **PRAISE REPORT!**

So many other great things happened in my life as a result of owning this store. One example is, while operating this store, I was approached by another young entrepreneur who had an idea to open the same type of store, but for children. She asked me to mentor her since my store was successful, and we were in no direct competition, not to mention that the marketing side aligned, as the foot traffic was a win for us both since she was exploring the same neighborhood location. This was an amazing opportunity to take what I had learned and share it for the betterment of others. And it worked. Although I no longer own the store, she has owned and operated hers for the last twenty-plus years, and I am most grateful to God for the experience and for the opportunity to be a blessing to her. **PRAISE REPORT!** And this comes with a lesson *to never be afraid to ask for help*. There are so many people out there who want to help, so being approached is absolutely the most streamlined ways to find those with a need.

Another is when I met an amazing woman with her own God-ordained testimony. She was another small business owner in the area and later in life, the mother of a famous NFL player, but he was only in college at that time. She was and is a beautiful Christian woman with an amazing story of her own survival, and the only thing I can share related to that is how God protected her and her son through devastating situations, and with her genuine love and prompting, God led their lives on to a victorious Journey. Her son now has an amazing platform and shares God's love and goodness as a testimony. **PRAISE REPORT!**

After several years into this Journey, I began a desire to go back to college and seek a business degree, as I already had earned an associate's degree in nutrition management, but I felt God tugging at my heart to go in another direction. But how could I run a business and take classes at the same time? I was at a crossroad. I began praying firmly for further direction, and of course, in God's way of directing us, there came the RATS. It sounds almost biblical, but yes, there was a neighborhood rat infestation that arrived shortly after the bakery on that block had been destroyed by a horrible fire. Later, we were to learn that the rats were feasting on the flour and sugar in the bakery basement.

This totally freaked me out because I bought bakery goods from that well-established, locally popular bakery for my seasonal fashion shows (one of my innovative ideas). The rats worked their way up the block, and my basement became infested. This was horrible because that was where I stored my costumes (another one of my innovative ideas), as I had postured myself as a local costumer for local high schools, college production, and dinner theater, thanks to one of my college professors at CCAC who reconnected with me after learning that I had opened my store, and he needed costumes. My store was helpful in this new endeavor of propelling me to becoming a costumer, and I loved it…probably because it did require other restore shopping to accommodate, but that was another area in which I was well versed. I love vintage clothing and accessories. This was another great GOD connection. He used my intrinsic areas of interests to accomplish His! **PRAISE REPORT!**

The rats began to infest my basement storage area, and unfortunately, any mitigation attempted, including a steel mesh wall, was not enough. One Saturday morning, I arrived at my store only to find a cat-sized rat on my show floor. That was not going to work. I could not risk my customers' safety and exposure. So prayerfully that very day, I closed my store. It was a tough decision, but a decision that later opened doors for me to take on another great growth and provisional opportunity with a local food manufacturing company who needed a professional administrative assistant for their Procurement Department. (It was so funny I had to look up the meaning of the word *procurement* before the interview.) But it is important to add that before the administrative assistant opportunity presented itself, I was offered a job at the local children's consignment store from the woman whom I helped mentor its opening, and I worked there for several months prior to getting the corporate position. It's so amazing to look back and see God's hand in every move I made at

that time—the perfect stepping stones to my next chapter of life.
PRAISE REPORT!

Years prior to my life-changing small business owner experience, when I was young and going through one of my two divorces and low on income, as I have mentioned, I was working several jobs, trying to further my education and taking care of babies. Times were tough. But looking back, I am grateful to this day that it worked out and I learned a lot through the process. One unique experience I remember clearest is when I had to get a lawyer to facilitate a much-needed divorce. My parents connected me with one close by in the area whom they had known from their business dealings. I met with him to discuss my situation, and he agreed to support from a legal perspective, although there was a fee. When I saw the fee on paper, my heart sunk. I knew I could not come up with $750. It may as well been $100,000 in my mind, as that was just a lot of money, or a lot of diapers, depending on your mindset!

I'm sure he saw the disappointment in my face, so I explained to him on the front end that I would need to make payments and asked for his alignment. He seemed to take on an empathy for my situation and said to me, "Someday you will be in a better situation, and when you are, you can pay me then." I couldn't believe my ears. Did he really say that? It took such a pressure off me, and I promised I would. I knew in my heart that I would be able to pay him back, not sure when... BUT SOMEDAY.

As I had not forgotten my promise and the gift he gave me that day, that someday came a few years later. I had received an income tax return in almost that same exact amount that I owed him, so I cashed it and paid the man. To this day, I believe that God honored that promise and my act to keep it and has blessed me fruitfully. **PRAISE REPORT!** But I also have learned from that event and look for the spirit of God to move me to helping others in the same way.

Yes, there was a lot of hard work and education behind what helped to facilitate that fruitful blessing, but He has ordained it and allowed me to bless others with some degree of prosperity. Ask God to impress upon your heart the desire to help others, to pay past debts, and to be fiscally honorable.

As a related callout, please know also that not every person who asks you for something is your responsibility. Be smart and keep your support most prayerfully led.

RECOMMENDATION: Start a prayer journal to not only track the prayers on your heart that you lift up to the Lord but more excitingly, to track how God answers them. Sometimes it's not what you expect. And talking about inspiration, it's an amazing exercise to keep you humbled yet inspired and equips you to share with others and inspire them!

To further demonstrate how God has His hand intertwined in my life, I want to share an interesting story that I entitled "A Sojourner's Story." It is about my mother-in-law Kay, whom I had the honor of knowing for the last five years and ten months of her life.

Of her almost seventy-nine years on earth, it is an amazing example of how God blessed me to share my life and faith with Kay. And He blessed her by taking her to glory in her time of suffering and need. For those five years, which now seem so short, I tried to share with her God's free gift of salvation. She was a long-standing Catholic woman and never had the experience of a personal relationship with the living God, but she did know everyone else in the church! She once referred to me as Preacher Wendy—but not in my presence, and when it was shared with me, I most definitely took that as a compliment.

I had many opportunities and could not stop sharing with her the life-changing Jesus I had come to know, love, and trust, and how He had actually worked in my own life, and the stories of His mercy and provision (You are reading some of them in this book).

I truly loved Kay. I put her on every prayer list I could find. She struggled with diabetes, cancer, and complications from the cancer treatment, including kidney failure, which required her to start dialysis treatment for approximately three years prior to her passing. My family and friends who attended a Tuesday morning prayer group at my mother's home lifted her up to God in prayer each week for a year. Kay actually did join us once at that prayer group, and I remember her only request to God was that He would not let her suffer if it was her time to die. Although Kay had heard the word of God and knew of Jesus, she did not have a living, intimate relationship. She never had the opportunity to allow His awesome power to change her own life—healing or no healing. Well, despite her previous situation, God heard and honored her heartfelt prayer when Kay was hospitalized in late December of 1997.

After being upgraded from a bout of pneumonia, she began to talk strangely. She mentioned on a phone conversation with me that she was going to die and didn't want the other family members to know. She said she heard the voices. But hours prior, it seemed she was getting well…and then throughout the course of that day, it seemed she was further losing her mental capacities. She was tucked into bed about 9:00 p.m. the evening of Sunday, January 4, 1998, only to be found the next morning in her hospital bed in a coma state, with her body violently shaking. After further conversations with her medical team, there seemed to be no known cause for these "tremors" that her body was experiencing. Later we would discover this was God's way of answering her prayer and captivating her mind to protect her from suffering and to prepare for His plan.

Her family, being predominantly Catholic, had called her parish for a priest to perform the honors of last rights, but he was not available to come to that hospital because it was not his designated "hospital for visitation." Let's forget the fact that she was a member of that church for the past fifty years and was a regular contributor… they should have supported this request, but they didn't, and needless to say, this was hard for the family to understand. And knowing that she needed prayer, *and most importantly for her salvation*, my husband and I insisted that our church pastor come to her aid in these critical moments (and the entire family's critical moments), as we were not sure if she was going to pass or come out of this comatose state. They all agreed.

Pastor Mike showed up within hours of our request. As the family stood holding hands around her bedside, he led a prayer in asking God that she have peace and then presented her while in her comatose state the opportunity to accept Jesus as her Savior. Immediately, her body became still, as if she accepted Him in that same moment, and for the next four days that she lay unconscious in a coma state, her body was relaxed. As we visited and spoke to her, we knew she could hear us. We talked to her, prayed for her, laughed, cried, read to her, and just loved her. By Friday, day five of the coma, her health had drastically declined, and her blood pressure was failing. We knew it would soon be time to say our final goodbyes.

As I left the hospital to pick up the kids from school that afternoon, I kissed her on her forehead and whispered in her ear, "Follow the light." I knew in my heart that I would not see her alive again on this earth, and that pain cut deep—deeper than I had ever experienced at this point in my lifetime. Kay left us that afternoon surrounded by her four children loving her and singing to her. That night was the hardest to get through, as that was my first experience with the death of someone whom I loved so closely, and it was hard for me to handle. She and I were like best friends. My husband held me, and we got through it together.

The next day, I was still hurting, and I cried out to God to confirm in my heart that her soul had arrived in heaven, as I just had to know. And He was faithful as He always is. Faster than ever, He led me to a prayer journal, one that was given to me that Christmas by my close friend Emma. And as I opened to the table of contents, there it was, as if in neon lights, the entry "Follow the Light"; and as I opened to it on page 145, I was enlightened by the words God placed before me. It read, John 8:12, "I am the light of the world; whoever follows me will never walk in darkness, but will have the light of life" and then I saw it. The words filled my soul with a joy that could only come from God. It read that the Christians in Ephesus were told that they were formerly in darkness but now are light in the Lord. **PRAISE REPORT!**

See, when I saw my mother-in-law alive for the last time, it was by request that I join my sister-in-law JoAnn in anointing Kay with holy water from Ephesus, Turkey, that JoAnn's friend had given to her, and we prayed with Kay too. At that time, I thought I was participating in this anointing for JoAnn's sake, but little did I know that this was all a part of God's plan for me too. He saw the big picture. God talked to me in a personal way through this experience…

one that could not be mistaken and was His way of giving me a total confirmation of His grace. He was letting me be certain! The pain and joy were so close that I could hardly hold back the tears, writing these nine days after her passing. It was all quite an emotional wave. Now, twenty-plus years later, I thank God to this day for giving me hope while here on earth, that I one day will again see her beautiful face, but with Jesus in heaven.

You see how important that initial step becomes when you witness someone you love come so close to missing their peaceful *Grand Finale*. It is my hope and prayer that this story demonstrates a compelling example of how God meets us in the very place we need to share His love with us. I wrote that story when this all happened, and adding it to this book has been a highlight of this share.

In the fifty-six years that God has allowed me to live and enjoy His blessings, I have experienced much—some good and some bad as I have already shared. I consider myself to be overqualified in human experiences, as most of us are, as far as experiences are concerned. The reason is because I have made some devastating choices in my lifetime, choices typically made in haste and without proper planning or counsel. Yes, I am impulsive, but I am learning that this gift can be used for good *but must be Spirit-led*. Before I knew Jesus, my decisions were certainly not Spirit-led and had resulted in some interesting and sometimes painful outcomes. And yet I would not have it any other way because I have made choices that yielded beautiful outcomes. Three of my biggest and best choices resulted in my three amazing sons and two stepsons.

Being Spirit-led is a true gift and can be as simple as the example I am about to share. I was in a thrift store shopping one afternoon, and while standing near this person who just began to check out, God's spirit clearly told me to pay for her items, but feeling like that was presumptuous, I hesitated. Then as I listened to the woman checking out (she was buying coats for her grandchildren), I overheard the cashier say, "I'm sorry, ma'am, but your card has been declined." I could tell she was taken by surprise. "Please run the card again. There must be some mistake," she responded. While the cashier began to rerun her card, I knew I had to act. I walked over and asked her if I could pay for her order, that it would be a blessing for me to be able to do that. She smiled and seemed a little confused…and then the cashier announced that the card was declined again. She looked at me and quietly said, "Thank you." I paid the cashier. And I knew the woman was grateful even though it wasn't for me to judge. I just needed to do what God prompted me to do, but she hugged me and said, "God bless you." And I told her He already had!

As I am writing this message over many years past, these types of stories have repeated throughout my life since learning to be attuned to Spirit-led direction. Many of my past decisions have not been Spirit-led and have caused me to make some interesting decisions. And as already shared, two of which are my two failed marriages and some events that occurred surrounding them. I realize that although I was not able to salvage them, as I chose to abandon them for what then was a good-enough reason for me, I thank God that He is a God of second, and sometimes third, or fourth, and fifth, and more chances.

I sometimes wonder if my choices had steered me from His perfect plan for my life, as perhaps a less painful plan? But I wouldn't change that for anything. Despite my having to live with and experience many consequences, He was still there with me through it all, perhaps not in His perfect will because I did not know how to listen to Him and let His spirit lead me. I was not walking with Him and communicating with Him daily. I was thinking about myself, sometimes in survival mode, and not what His will was at that time. But He watched over me still and let me learn in my time…and His loving heart, and as I have learned His sense of humor, He used those consequences to my greatest benefit. Because that's what He does. He makes great things out of our mistakes, just like the character of God to make good out of seemingly bad situations. I do admit that it took me a bit of time throughout my life to see all the blessings that were before me. In retrospect, it is much clearer now to see the blessings, but that is usually the case. And later in my life, to better understand what I learned through all of those experiences. One thing is for sure, that you should never judge a book by its cover. You know what I mean!

One of my biggest blessings is my first and eldest of three sons. He is a result of my first marriage when I was eighteen years old. The child who survived being by my side through many years of my own growing up. And then five years later, my second greatest blessing, my middle child and second son from marriage number two, was born. The marriages definitely resulted in two of my biggest blessings! God gave me two of my greatest gifts not as a stumbling block to my own life's agenda, but as gifts to help me stay dependent upon Him and to teach me the skill of being a mother with true compassion and genuine love.

If asked when the actual day I was saved by God's grace, I would say it was many years back, when I was just a child. I was about eleven years old when my parents "hauled" me and my siblings to a Bible-believing, Jesus-loving church in Allison Park. At this church, they preached the message of salvation. This was something I had not previously heard in our regular Catholic church service. If it was preached, I never heard it. This experience was so impactful to my family that even after forty-plus years, my mother still remembers the beautiful song that was being sung during that altar call: "Jesus. Jesus. Jesus. There is something about that name."

The point is that we all accepted Jesus as our Lord and Savior that one day. We answered an altar call and prayed a prayer from our hearts that God would be in *us*. And to this day, although I was young, I remember this happening. I know the decision I made. But there is also sadness in this memory. It's that we left that church too soon, before having the opportunity to learn more about God and establish a personal relationship with Him. It was my dad's idea and stern decision, as he was offended by the pastor on a cold, snow-covered day. See, we drove through brutal winter weather to attend Sunday morning service, only to be told upon arrival that the service was canceled. But we made the trip from a bit of a distance, and the minister had made a prior promise that the "show would go on" no matter how many people were able to attend. But it didn't, and we were history.

I regretted my dad's prideful decision that winter morning, but my heavenly Father honored the commitments of our hearts. We fell away from Jesus as a family for many years, so we stopped getting fed and, ultimately, stopped growing closer to God. The joyous part of this story is that although we continued on the road of life not fully honoring our commitment, He did not forget about us and His commitment.

Later in life, I was reconnected with God via a friend I met in junior college. She invited me to church, and when I attended, I immediately knew I was "home." This is when I started to recommit, and the joy in my Journey was made real. I am not suggesting it takes a church community to support your relationship with God, but the church and the people who love Jesus are witnesses, such as the stories written in this book, and support your personal Journey in love, encouragement, and most importantly, getting to learn God's Word and His promises.

I have had the opportunity to now only attend Christian churches, but I did experiment with other types of religions along my Journey to really learn for myself. I will save those stories for another day and another time, but the essence of what I am trying to convey is that whatever it takes to get you there, it's worth every second, hour, day, year. My hope is that the words shared in this book help to get YOU there sooner so you can reap the benefits and become not only a blessing in your life but to others in need.

All of my immediate family members now know and have experienced the power found in having a personal relationship with Jesus. Again, God honored our heartfelt prayers as youth. For the men in my family, it may have taken a bit longer. They had to relinquish some of their control, so I get it to some regard, but they have also witnessed God's power and that helped to make the difference. I truly thank God for every courageous man out there, having found the freedom in giving God the place of authority in their lives and in their homes.

I took a trip out of state, which required me to fly on two planes to reach my destination. I did not anticipate flying, nearly as much as the destination, because I was going to visit my friend Emma. I did not like to fly. I'd rather have myself on the ground, if you know what I mean. I dislike flying to the extent that I made a trip to the health store earlier that day to get something to keep me calm through the experience and found some homeopathic calming tablets (Calms Forte). It was stated on the guidelines that you only needed about three of these tablets to cure insomnia. Well, I was on my fifth tablet and was wide awake.

As the plane taxied down the runway, there was a delay in take-off announced. *Isn't this just great?* I thought, with more anticipation and also a great opportunity to get introduced to my flying neighbor in seat 7A on this Boeing 747. *How brave he must be*, I thought. Sitting next to the window, and so calm, I actually thought he was sleeping. "I hope my snoring doesn't bother you," he stated unexpectedly. I looked over and chuckled. "Actually, it makes me feel right at home," I replied. That was the icebreaker for my new friend Tom. We ended up talking the entire trip, and it turned out that he was a believer too, and we had a lot in common. I shared that I was writing a book (this book!), and how God was going to use my writing to encourage other women. But as I spoke, it wasn't difficult for him to figure out my irritation with the flying situation. The expressions on my face when experiencing pressure changes was proof enough, not to mention the stutter in my voice during those turbulent episodes. He began to explain air pressure and other technical things about the safety of flying, but I found no comfort.

I guess it wasn't enough to put up with me that entire flight to Chicago. We were then informed that the plane could not land for at least another thirty minutes due to air traffic. Well, I never experienced a traffic jam in outer space before, so I guess that made me a bit more tense. It was so noticeable that Tom then asked me another question. "So, Wendy, who is flying this plane?" *How am I supposed to know the pilot?* I thought. "Gee, Tom, I don't know the pilot." It turned out that Tom did know the pilot. "God is flying this plane," he said. "And what good does it do to worry and wonder what could happen to you up here in this plane when ultimately God is in control? So don't worry. When you get frightened by flying, just remember who's flying the plane."

Now folks, I thought I realized this in every area of my life, from finances to baking a cake, but put me in a big metal plane and throw me in a cloud puff and I can't think straight. But God was faithful as He always is. He put Tom, a man with my dad's name, in row seven (God's number), who snores like my husband, to get my perspective straight. You can't imagine how much more comfortable that made me, flying back home a few days later. I even sat next to the window. This is an amazing example of how God uses committed Christians to help others in all situations, and me in this seemingly silly situation. God is faithful. **PRAISE REPORT!**

Tom and I parted with a handshake and a "God bless," and he will probably never know the true impact he made on my life that afternoon. His words of wisdom have been used in my life on many more occasions actually. I have learned to incorporate them into my daily living—when fear tries to creep back into my mind. I reassure myself that "God's flying this plane."

Tom was committed to the Lord. He shared pictures of his family, his wife and two sons, and spoke about the Bible. He felt comfortable sharing with me on a spiritual level. I can't help but have respect for men like Tom. **PRAISE REPORT!**

Thank you, Tom, for being the God-loving man that you are!

Chapter O = Openness...
Let God Lead You

✦

The *O* in *Journey* represents our openness to God and His Word—to be as a child and demonstrate openness to God's leading, otherwise referred to as obedience. But to be open to obedience in the first place, you have to know how to listen to God's direction.

What rules your life, your decisions, your actions?

At a high level, when you think of obedience, you're really thinking about obeying the "rules." There are certainly benefits to being open and obedient to God. I once read a quote by Joyce Meyer that stated, "Obedience to God is the pathway to the life you really want to live." As shared already, I have experienced this personally and am grateful.

John 14:15 states that if we truly love God, we will keep His commandments.

If you are a parent or have one yourself, think about why there are rules in your home. Typically, rules are put in place to keep you safe. How frustrating it is when our kids break our rules and end up getting hurt, breaking something, hurting a sibling, or just paying for it in some other way. You don't want to see them go through that, but as I think about it, sometimes that is what it takes for them to learn why you made the rules in the first place.

Later in that passage in John 14:23, Jesus stated that "anyone who loves me will obey my teachings." Living in obedience can be a lifelong struggle, and I have met folks who have experienced just that. But I have also learned that the more you experience opportunities, the stronger your ability to act on them more appropriately becomes.

I equate the word *obedience* with openness or conviction. When you feel conviction deep in your heart, it is not judgment. God does not judge you, so why do you judge others? It is God's voice guiding you to change, a change that will bring joy. See, God is a loving heavenly Father, not a judge trying to convict you. He knows we are not perfect, that's why we need Jesus. He knows because He ordained Jesus to us!

The end product of having a personal relationship with God and seeking His will in your life is to allow the possibilities that God can influence your choices and decisions. He sees the big picture. We don't always have that same opportunity. Our closeness to God is what gives us confidence.

Confidence is different from conscience, as this is typically developed according to what you have learned from your environment and your past—what you have experienced growing up and the influences of others. Living with these influences typically left me with self-induced problems because they were a result of my then-self-seeking mindset. I didn't know that at the time, but even when I learned that things could be different by seeking God's will, it took me many years of trial and error to step out in faith and give it over to God. LIVE & LEARN!

Read Romans 8:28 and be assured that God sees the outcome where we see the problem.

This is where trust plays a part. To obey, you have to TRUST the one making the rules. Trust typically requires unanswered questions, and as Joyce Myers would say "get comfortable with that."

There are two interesting, related stories that come to mind to this regard that are definitely worth sharing.

I vividly remember watching an episode of *Walker, Texas Ranger* many years back where a young girl, I would say she was about eight to ten years old, stood up to the thugs in her "dangerous" neighborhood. It was titled "Little Miracle in the Hood." Even at that young age, she was so connected with God and was open to standing up for what was right. It turned out this little girl made a significant impact on her community by being courageous and following God's lead to do what was right—where even adults feared to tread. I realize this is a TV show, but I can't help but appreciate the message of courage and how her courageous steps in obedience and faith made a significant positive impact.

The other story is true and directly impacted my being able to complete this book because of a recent company downsizing experience. Being released from my position or eliminated is something I had never experienced in my professional career and honestly never wanted to, but it has turned out to be the biggest blessing for me personally. It has allowed me the freedom to finish the book that God has envisioned for me to complete—this book!

Am I uncertain about the usefulness and impact this book will make on its readers? (Yes) Am I uncertain about my future career? (Yes) Am I uncertain about how I will continue to generate provision for my family? (Yes) But this is the beauty of trusting God because he who began a good work in me, will be faithful to complete it.

I am using this time to reevaluate my professional self. What do I want to do for the next ten to fifteen years professionally? It's for sure a purging and refining process. God definitely got my attention but also provided for me along the way. I am completing this book, and what's next in my future has not yet been defined; but I am excited to learn more on how I will be restored in my procurement career or elsewhere once this book is shared. After all, this was a vision He gave to me. **PRAISE REPORT!**

As shared, openness is ultimately being open spiritually and emotionally to where the Lord is leading us. This then evolves into obedience, and this word has always been a difficult one for me. As I mentioned before, I am impulsive. I can take responsibilities for my actions, but my actions are not always well planned. Even as a teenager, I bucked authority—the typical rebel child I was. From the time I was sixteen (probably younger, but I couldn't do much about it), I decided that I knew what was best for me. I also had low self-esteem, which didn't help me any. Actually, it helped me to choose friends who were not good examples, and I fell into the trap of drug experimentation. I defied my parents' judgment and set out on a path of destruction. Before graduating from high school, I was living on my own. With a history of *disobedience* that goes back to high school, you can imagine how difficult I found it to be obedient to God, a God I could not see or hear. As much as I tried to learn and grow, I just couldn't get that obedience thing right.

As I also shared earlier, my second marriage was what I thought as an act of obedience. It turned out to be bad judgment. Staying celibate until the wedding, I could not bring myself to sleep with him afterward. But I trusted and obeyed and then woke up to what seemed to be a bad reality show. This was not for me. Then I questioned everything in my life. I turned my back from trusting God. How could He have allowed me to make such a mistake? But I did make that decision knowing in my heart it was not right for me and later realized I was following man's leading and not God.

And there I was, thinking if my way was wrong, and supposedly God's way was wrong, what was right? Nothing in my life had seemed to be right at this point, and I could not imagine it ever being right. Now I was really in a situation. From there, I went doing it my way again. At least if I did it my way, I would feel better about taking the responsibility for my own actions. From that point, I endeavored into life with an attitude of looking out for myself, since no one else would.

Obedience doesn't necessarily have to look you in the face of such devastating issues. There are smaller issues in one's life that must be thought out as well, like your day-to-day decisions of what TV programs are acceptable and what time management areas need to be established for your good as well as your family's. How about the music that you listen to? Did you know that your eyes and ears are the passageways to your soul…and what you put in them becomes a part of you? And that can have both positive and negative effects. Which do you choose? And why are these seemingly innocent areas affecting us? God's Word addresses every area of our lives. It is so important to spend time getting to know and understand it. It's in the Holy Bible. I personally refer to the Bible as God's Instructional Handbook for Life. If we choose to seek His direction, He will reveal it to us. That is where this becomes obedience—walking in the path of His wisdom and direction.

I was interviewing a young wife and mother from the Chicago area for this book, and as we talked, she mentioned that after becoming a Christian, she was compelled to make some serious changes to the decor of her home. At that time, I honestly was not seeing the connection of how your home decor could have any effect on your Christian walk. She explained to me that as she had established a closer walk with Jesus, she felt that she had no business decorating her home with things such as dream catchers and other superstitious items or items from other religions, like Buddha dolls for example. Have you seen these in a professing Christians home? She had a good point; she explained that our children need to see our home as a safe place that is reflective of our faith, not things that contradict them. We should make our homes warm and inspiring for our family, keeping in mind that this will surely reflect in their personality and self-image.

RECOMMENDATION: If you need help finding affordable inspirational home decor, check out the P. Graham Dunn store in Dalton, Ohio, or online. They are a faith-based manufacturer of so many inspirational items, including personalized gifts. More notably, they are recognized for their puzzle piece picture frames that can also be personally inscribed. As a customer of theirs who has my family framed in my entranceway to welcome my guests into a homier feel, I appreciate this company and the positive energy I get when I visit their showroom. At a recent visit for a book signing, I realized they had a Prayer & Praise Wall in the front of their retail store. Now, that's how you do it my friend!

As a young mother, I personally knew little about making a home a warm atmosphere. Home for me was where you were when you weren't everywhere else. I worked several jobs, so it made sense. After closing my unique resale shop, I had the opportunity to make some modifications to my home. I focused on putting more effort into actually cleaning it, and then I made some steps toward organizing, followed up by a few personal touches around the home in general (wall art, family portraits, floral sprigs, a fresh coat of paint). WOW, with just these minimal changes, my home actually felt more comfortable. Some might say it was warmer. How interesting and grateful I was when my mother visited shortly after I had made those changes and commented, "Wendy, I'm not sure what it is, but your home feels much warmer and more comfortable to be in." That, my friend, was a huge compliment coming from my mother. She must have learned that early in life because she always prioritized keeping her house very homey and clean as we were growing up. This is such a warm memory for me.

I have, over the years, began to collect angels, a collection that was actually influenced by my mother, as she gave all of her children an angel ever year for Christmas to hang on our tree. When the season was over, I took down all the angels I had to that point and found them a new and special place throughout my home. I just wanted to be surrounded by God's angels all year long. It's something that personally gives me peace, adds to the comfort of my home, and serves as a daily reminder that God is watching over me and my family.

Let's face it, obedience is also very closely tied to our attitude—a decision we make every day. And attitude is 90 percent of your mindset and outlook. How is your language expressed at home in front of your children or your spouse? Does it reflect your love for God, or your rebellious spirit? Let yourself be spiritually led in all situations, especially in anger. I realize this is a tough thing to do when tempers flare for reasons that seem justifiable, but remind yourself what this local company here in Perry Township, Ohio, shared. As they are a company that is not afraid to profess their trust in God, they recently posted on their marquee: "A Gentle Answer Deflects Anger, but Harsh Words Make Tempers Flare."

> Let no corrupt communication proceed out
> of your mouth, but that which is good to the use
> of edifying, that it may minister grace unto the
> hearers. (Ephesians 4:29)

Remember to "count it all joy," as shared in James 1:2, when you have a situation and need to obey God. In the fifth chapter of Luke, we were given an example of how obedience works. When Jesus told the fishermen to let down their nets, they assured Him that they fished all night, and no fish were to be found. But in obedience, they let down their nets, and they were then filled abundantly. We should learn through this Bible story that as much as we try to take things into our own hands and in our own strength, we will get nothing spiritual to show for it unless it is ordained by God for us to do so. Don't wait until you've tried, tried, and tried again and still can't get it right. Give it to God first and allow His power to get it right for you, maybe not the first time, but even if you fall short, you will know it was by divine appointment.

If you know it is a vision or direction from God, NEVER GIVE UP! What could be just around your corner?

The Bible verse Matthew 5:16 reminds me of a children's song that I learned as a child that is a true guide to staying positive. I'm sure you have heard of it too. It goes, "This little light of mine, I'm gonna let it shine, let it shine, let it shine, let it shine!" We all need to SHINE or learn how to SHINE. The verse literally states that we should let our light shine before others so they can see the good in you and how that glorifies God. It's no wonder my favorite word in life has always been *shine!*

Always be OPEN to the positive that is in your life already and that God can bring into your future; for example, good health, prosperity, sharing, giving, supporting, mentoring, and showing compassion and courtesy when you can. God can bring all these good things into your life by knowing and then exercising His encouragement that comes from the Spirit-led words found in the Bible (Ten Commandments, Bible stories, Jesus's life examples, Bible promises, etc.). These are what prompt our visions and convictions. Read them, put them into practice. Responding and acting upon His word is your best path. And yes, this can be painful at times, but the victory comes in trusting and obeying His direction *for your life specifically.* You will only know this by building a personal relationship with our living God.

If you recall the lawyer story I shared in Chapter J, blessings abound when you pay your debts and give all the glory to God for making it possible. In an interesting time in these world happenings, as we are all looking for answers, keep in mind that the Bible, or what I call God's Instructional Handbook for Life, provides us with edification and direction. I see and hear it on the news, commercials, and talk shows daily about the depression and anxiety that everyone is experiencing. Go to your Maker and let Him ease your soul during this crazy time.

Openness and obedience to God's prompting is essential to keep our relationship with God strong throughout our Journey. It's the positive energy that keeps our actions in step with God's plan. Jesus performed miracles when He was on earth. There are many examples in the Bible where He fed the hungry, healed the sick, and even brought the dead back to life in certain circumstances. We need to have a miracle mindset in our lives because knowing and loving and being open to the Lord Jesus is the opportunity to allow miracles happen.

I heard a sermon a couple years ago by a pastor at the Log Church in Pittsburgh. It was around this idea that we need to have a miracle mindset. The story shared was about the time that God fed the thousands who were gathered with Him and they ran out of food, but He used the lunch of a young boy to multiply it and feed them all. Who would have ever thought that could happen? There were three things about that sermon that stuck out to me and still keep top of mind to this day:

1. TRUST in Jesus to deliver a miracle in His way, in His time, and for His purpose (think of the Joni Eareckson Tada story). Do not entertain a defeated mindset. It's like pouring out the negative energy and inviting it back to you. Never give up or get discouraged, depressed, or broken. Our God is LIMITLESS, so DREAM BIG.

2. OPENNESS to OBEDIENCE is critical (Luke 9:14–15). When you are open in your relationship with God by prayer and daily conversation, He provides you with direction by moving your heart in kindness and goodness. FOLLOW YOUR HEART. Act on His prompting, as this is the key to unlocking God's miracles in your life and for using you perhaps to unlock miracles in others' lives. Don't

be self-defeating and talk yourself out of it. GO WITH YOUR GOD-GIVEN GIFTS. Pray for vision and direction daily. I have heard limitless stories about others who have been in need, as well as my own, and God moved someone to reach out to them to provide a meal, money, miscellaneous needed items, and so forth. It's amazing to be a part of the divine intervention whether you are the giver or the receiver. Do what you need to do, but let God be totally in control.

3. BE THANKFUL always (John 6:11). Let's face it, if you are alive today and reading this book, you are amazingly blessed. We need to thank God every day for what we have. Remember, we can work daily and do all the things we need to do to maintain our position or role, but ultimately, God is in control. Work like it's in your hands and pray to God, knowing it is all in His.

    AND PRAY WITH AUTHORITY. You
    are a child of the Almighty God!

Chapter U = Unique Usefulness

✦

Usefulness can be described as exactly what it says, so how can God use you? How does God use others? The answers to these questions can go on forever.

The truth is that God uses us all in varying ways. Sometimes we can have our spiritual eyes opened to see the way God is using us, and at other times we don't even know that He did. This is why it is so important to be attuned to the leading that God places on your heart. He uses us to broaden His kingdom, to help others who are in need or struggling, to brighten someone's day, OR TO CHANGE THE WORLD! The ways God uses us is endless if we are open to His prompting.

Here's an interesting story about exactly that. My friend Christine recently shared this story with me. It's about her being given an opportunity to be used by God in another person's life. She was personally planning a trip to travel to an edification seminar, and while praying much about the event, it was put on her heart for another person she knew, a colleague, to attend with her. But when she approached the other person about attending, they were greatly interested but could not afford the cost to make the trip. This prompted Christine to pray a great deal about this situation because she just knew her friend had to attend because she was given a message and believed this was what God wanted. Therefore, she knew He would somehow and someway provide. She decided to step out in faith. Even though she was not financially able to support both, she paid for the trip, trusting God would provide because after all, He had put this in her heart to make sure she and her friend attended. Soon after arriving back home from the trip, she was given an unexpected bonus at work for the exact amount to cover all the travel cost. **PRAISE REPORT!**

God uses our weaknesses to magnify his strength. HOW IS GOD USING YOU?

Galatians 5:13 (LB) reads, "Dear brothers, you have been given freedom: not freedom to do wrong, but freedom to love and serve each other." FREE WILL, use it wisely!

How about the recent emergence of random acts of kindness? I love these. I recently viewed a YouTube video. It showed a young woman helping a blind Chicago Cub's fan who was having trouble calling a taxi on the street after the game. She was an onlooker who stopped what she was doing and took time out of her life to help him out. Is that something you would do? I hope that is something we would all do. Let others see God in YOU! There are many ways this can be accomplished in a heartfelt manner: bake cookies for a neighbor, give a grocery cart to another shopper, pay forward for a drive-through order, make dinner for a family in need, insert coins in an expired parking meter, leave coins in a vending machine, and the list could go on forever. We can all be examples of the living God and His work. It actually draws others closer.

We are God's heart beating in our own communities. We don't know the time or place that God will use us, but the important thing is that we are open to His usefulness when and where the opportunity arises. We are also unique. This uniqueness is a gift! In my exposure of God's amazing utilization of His people, I see that He uses us in areas that we are different so we can touch many.

This leads to five areas I would like to explore with you, which are aligned to usefulness. Anyone who knows me knows that I take seriously the 4 *E*'s and a *P* of business, as they are an important approach in recruiting top talent. In this same sense, I believe the following five areas are the most important in all of our lives, but with a twist—4 *P*'s and an *E*:

The first area is PURPOSE. Start each new
day with a sense of purpose. Be thankful for the

loved ones in your life, for what you have, or sometimes for what you don't have. Gratitude and a positive attitude aren't always easy to convey but are strong forces. Remember Romans 8:28: "And we know that all things work together for Good for those who love the Lord, those who are called according to His purpose."

The second area is PASSION. What are you passionate about? Tap into those God-given predispositions. When you are passionate about something, that means you will have a far greater impact when demonstrating support regardless of what that action of support entails.

The third area is PRIORITIES. Sometimes this means moving your schedule to accommodate another person's needs, or even canceling a planned event. To this you must be prayerful and intuitive. Moreover, you need to be attuned in your relationship with God, allowing Him to direct you. The only way I know to get to this space is by prayer and praise, reading God's Word, talking to God about anything and sometimes everything.

The fourth area is PLAN. Being in God's plan is the best thing you will ever experience. Just knowing He has a plan for you can be the most encouraging thing for your own self-actualization. God has a plan for all of our lives. He wants to see us prosper. This has many meanings, my friend—grow, thrive, succeed, enjoy provision, and the like. As Proverbs 3 shares, we must trust in Him, and He will make our path straight. (Proverbs 3:5–7 reads, "Trust in the LORD with all thine heart; and lean not unto thine own understanding. In all thy ways acknowledge him, and he shall direct thy paths.")

Reflecting back on my own Journey and the birth of my second son, as I shared, he was born with a late gestational diaphragmatic hernia; and although I do not know how God allowed that to happen, I believe it resulted from a situation where I was helping another person. I was working at my ex-in-laws' deli, and one day my ex-husband's girlfriend had stopped in for lunch. I was glad to be in a different situation, so her presence did not bother me in the least bit. In fact, when she began to choke on her lunch, I was the first one to run to her aid. Being trained in first aid since grade school, I performed the Heimlich maneuver on her, and immediately, the ball of ham that was lodged in her throat came shooting out across the room. This happened at about eight and a half months into my pregnancy, *after the sonogram.* I can't be certain, but looking back on this situation, I'm thinking that this act of kindness and the pressure of performing the maneuver is what caused the baby's hernia. Some might say that is terrible, but I DO NOT. God certainly used this for the good. He used this to allow me to not only help another human being escape choking to death but to also change my adoption position aligned to my promise to my mother. Raising my son has been an amazing blessing overall, not to mention how that experience helped me to collectively grow as a person and a mother and to help others in similar situations along the path of life. **PRAISE REPORT!**

Add into your PLAN perspective and visualize your success and how might God use that for His good. Pray for vision. As shared, I have personally done this, and God has always exceeded my expectations, not for the purpose of greed or self-worthiness but to be a beacon of light. We are ALL worthy—never forget that! It's more around consciously taking the steps to align to Gods perfect will. Because we are not, or will never be, perfect, and oh, what a relief in knowing that!

Proverbs 29:18 states that without vision, God's people will perish.

On to the fifth area of ENCOURAGEMENT. All the *P*'s shared lead up to this *E*. God uses these steps to lead us in using our experiences to encourage others, and as I have learned on many occasions, to encourage ourselves along the way.

The main point is to seek God's will and be responsive to his Holy Spirit's prompting. This can only be performed as a result of your personal relationship with Jesus. Act upon it when your heart knows it's from Him. If you know that it is made with truth and love, make the effort, and you will see God revealing Himself through it.

As another example, many years ago, I asked God to use me and was impressed to start a prayer cell group in my home. But I didn't want to give over my home, as I was self-conscious of its condition even though I knew in my heart and accepted that my home was a gift from God. It was an act of obedience to be used. And oh, the blessings from acting on God's prompting were uncountable, by just stepping out in faith. I had to remember that God will never ask you to do something contradictory to His word. Be Spirit-led. Stay in touch and in tune with God and you will feel His prompting. And then listen and act on His prompting. This is how He uses us to bless others, by our openness. He blesses us when we are being obedient.

Our usefulness is an important part of our individual Journey. This is the willingness to be used by God in any arena or area of your life. It can be as simple as saying a prayer for another person's needs, making a cup of tea for another, or lending a listening ear.

Several years ago, God once again used me to open my home for prayer for women interested in praying for each other. Several women from my church attended, and we were prayer partners. We journaled our prayer requests and praises. I knew that God asked me to facilitate this union. He stirred it in my heart for many months. And when I opened my doors, each chair was filled. There were so many prayers answered and hearts warmed by each other's care, all in the name of Jesus. And I found it interesting that as a confirmation of this willingness to engage in the name of Jesus, and of its effectiveness for God's kingdom, I was faced with what I refer to as spiritual battles: like a broken water line (on the city side, thank God), an ant infestation, and even an eviction notice. And as if that wasn't embarrassing enough, there was the RAT—yes, my house was graced by the presence of a really big and smart rat. It seemed once I decided to be useful and use my home as a house of prayer, the opposition tried many tricks to keep my home closed and unavailable. But God prevailed, and in no time, all of those issues were resolved. I want to comment that when the will of God is being fulfilled and positive impacts are being evidenced, one way or another, the devil tries his best at giving us a hard time. This story is a great example.

Again, usefulness is acting upon that small, still voice you have in your heart that by staying close in your relationship with Jesus, you know and understand it is from Him. God prompts you to do something. It may be to make a monetary or physical donation; it may be to volunteer as a Sunday school teacher or a nursery worker or a scrapbook teacher at a support program. Whatever it may be, you better believe you will be blessed for being a blessing to others.

Know that this can exhibit itself many ways. As there was once a time when I had a friend reach out to me, and although they didn't directly ask me for money, they told me they were in a situation, and they needed money to get out of that situation. With my giving spirit, I had to pray about it very seriously for days before handing over the cash, as something inside me was just not feeling right about sharing this with this person at this time. I struggled with it, but then I was enlightened. God definitely showed me that my heart's prompting to not share at that time was the right thing. God had other plans for this situation, I suppose.

Here's another interesting story: My mother took an evangelist class at her church. She was seriously wanting to be used by God, and after a great deal of prayer and conversations with God, she felt that this was a calling for her to participate in actual "feet on the street" ministry.

After weeks of training, this church established a team headed out to the streets, the streets of New York City, that is…in the chilling cold of winter. They started their outreach by doing a skit to gain passersby's attention. This was what opened a door for them to share the good news of Jesus. This trip was not for pleasure or dining or theater; it was an uncomfortable van trip with a mission and a message.

Sometimes we are asked to do uncomfortable things, but if they are instilled in our hearts, we must do them and not rob others of their blessing. Many souls met Jesus or rededicated themselves to Jesus that weekend through that encounter.

And although most rewarding, if that wasn't uncomfortable enough, their next adventurous outreach was in downtown Pittsburgh on New Year's Eve. At that event, they postured and manned a prayer station. They stood on the corners of the city during the New Year's Eve festivities and offered to pray with and for others and their needs. This is an amazing example of selfless giving. Giving of your time, energy, and comforts to share the free gift of salvation with genuine love. Remember, salvation is a gift from God and not an earned qualification, so this act was a gift from that mission team's heart as a directive from the Lord above. As shared, many times, being useful means stepping out of your comfort zone.

Many years back, I had an opportunity to reconnect with one of my first childhood friends. It was a random meet on the streets in the city of Pittsburgh, and it warmed my heart to see her. We talked for just a few moments that afternoon but shared contact information. It was shortly after that when I was led to reach out to her to truly connect. And when we finally did, I learned that she was living in one of the worst neighborhoods in the city with the highest crime rate—kind of scary. She had three beautiful young daughters and was in a bad financial situation. It broke my heart to see her struggling, especially since she had also experienced some mixed abuse scenarios, which played part into her being in this situation and also being a single parent.

At that point, I was not financially abundant, and all I had to offer her was prayer and a listening ear. And as I committed to praying for her, one day, the Lord spoke to my heart specifically as to how I could be a blessing to her family—yes, me with very limited resources at that time. It was getting closer to the holiday season, and it was impressed upon me to tap into my group of committed friends, prayer partners, and family to collect donations to potentially brighten this family's holiday.

This is when I sprang into action and specifically asked for clothing, food, household items, gift cards, and the like. And in three days, I had five lawn bags full of items including clothes and home goods, as well as money and gift cards. The thought was to surprise her with these gifts one afternoon after confirming she was home. When I arrived at her house, she came out to greet me. When I told her about the gifts that I had collected for her family, she broke out in tears. This was something she so desperately needed, and at a critical time in her life. I was crying too, mostly for her grateful spirit and openness to accept the gifts but also because there is such an amazing feeling to know you are in God's will and making a difference in someone's life.

What's your comfort zone? Who controls your limits? Is it you, or is it God?

Looking back on my life, I have so many stories of my being led out of my comfort zone, but when they were happening, it's like I almost didn't feel that way…well, kind of, sort of.

When my kids were young, I liked to dress them up in costumes to take them out shopping with me (Superman, Power Rangers, Peter Pan…you name it)—whatever made them feel special. This aided in my getting things accomplished, especially grocery shopping.

One day when at Kroger, which was not my regular grocery store (I just went there for some specials), I met an elderly woman who was in need of a ride back to her apartment, and her scheduled ride did not show up. She stopped me and asked for a ride because she could not carry her purchases. Since it was right around the corner, I agreed. So I packed up the kids and the groceries in my little Chevy Chevette and drove her over to her apartment.

As a sidebar, this was the car that my sister *gave* to me because she was blessed with another car unexpectedly, so she gave hers to me because I was bussing it around with my kids in tow. What an amazing blessing to be able to help others with a gift that was given to me! Yet another **PRAISE REPORT!**

When we arrived at her building, she asked if I could help her take the items up to her apartment. Feeling as though I should be helpful, I unpacked the kids from the car and grabbed her groceries, and we trekked up many flights of steps to get the bags delivered and get her settled. As we were heading up to her apartment, she asked me if I had ever been to a food bank before, and I had not. She told me about this great food bank not far from where I lived at the time actually. It was in the basement of a church, and they were incredibly giving. I took her phone number, and we connected shortly after. For about the next two years, I was her food bank buddy, and it definitely worked out for the both of us because I was in need at the time as well. WOW. What a powerful story of God's hand in motion. To be a blessing with no preconceived notions or expectations and get an amazing blessing back. That food bank *was* extremely generous, and at times, we had to stand outside in line to wait our turn, but it was a huge help—absolutely uncomfortable, but a true blessing.

One part of that story I was going to leave out is that this little old woman had a walker, and she herself moved especially slow, and anyone who knows me knows that I move fast. So this was definitely a lesson in patience. And the other part of the story is that she may not have taken a bath in a very long time. The scent was evident. I certainly had to step out of my comfort zone to help this woman, but God had put this in my care. SOMETIMES WE HAVE TO STEP OUT OF OUR COMFORT ZONE when God is calling us to action.

And speaking of stepping out of my comfort zone, I would include a story about helping out a man who lived near the river. I met him when I worked at a deli near the old Three Rivers Stadium. He was a different person in a lot of ways, kind of strange but personable. He had talked to me at times at the deli, which gave me a few opportunities to share with him my relationship with God. This led him to want to go to church. I told him about the great church I had just found on the other side of the city, and we agreed that I would pick him up one Sunday morning to attend with me.

On that day, I went to pick him up and knocked on his door. He answered and stated he just needed a minute, so I stood outside; and as I inadvertently got a glimpse inside his apartment, all I could see was roaches all over the place—crawling on the walls, the furniture, and the floor. It was honestly one of the worst things I have ever seen from an insect perspective in my life. It made me cringe. My impulse was to run away and apologize later. Instead, I quickly prayed for an answer. I ended up taking him to church and, needless to say, privately praying the entire time that I would not get roach transfer into my car. And lo and behold, he accepted Jesus at that church service. When I drove him home that day, we laughed, cried, and prayed along the way. Shortly after that interesting experience, I had not seen him around the deli and only much later learned that he had passed away. **PRAISE REPORT!**

I'm not sure how I would have felt had he missed that opportunity. Step out of your comfort zone. See others as Jesus, like Mother Teresa for example. She did not claim to see Jesus in herself; she saw the face of Jesus in every face she met along the way.

Think of your weakness as God's strength. This is a gift to open God's power in your life and bring us closer to God. I'm not suggesting that we remain weak in all aspects of our lives. We just need to be the best we can, knowing that God is our ultimate strength.

I sometimes reflect back on my personal experiences in my lifetime and how they have shaped me into the strong, independent businesswoman that I am today—Sunday school teacher/mentor/volunteer. Who would have thought these experiences would shape not only my personality but also my career!

And perhaps now a new career…

Chapter R = Relationships

✦

When I married the love of my life, we decided to write our own wedding vows. Well, I decided, and he agreed. WOW, what an amazing gift that was to each other! I want to share what my husband wrote to me as an example of how our relationship was founded on the full alignment with the love of God.

> Dear Wendy, my love, may the love we share today be even more important tomorrow. The happy times we've had and the not-so-happy times we made it through be a stepping stone to growing together. I vow to be faithful. I will respect you through good times and bad. Be beside you through sickness and health. Be there whenever you need me—I will love you until the day I die. I open my eyes, my heart, my soul and ask you, with Jesus as my witness, to be my wife, always and forever.

Is that powerful or what? I am reminded of these commitments every day because many years ago, I typed, printed, and framed them, and they are sitting on each of our bedsides; and honestly, that's a commitment that he has lived up to. We've have had our share of good and bad times for sure. And he has stood beside me throughout several health issues (including my brain tumor, which was a biggie) and career moves, to the point that he even retired early and relocated to another state to allow me to grow in my professional endeavors. That's true love.

With that, as important as our earthly relationships are, we need to get to a point when we realize that the single most important relationship we have should be with our Savior—Jesus Christ. With God as our Creator, who then would be the best counselor?

It is from this relationship that all other relationships should be founded. And through the interview process of writing this book, I have learned that in most situations, our closeness with God is reflected in most of our earthly relationships.

As all relationships first begin from an introduction, this pure introduction to Jesus is sometimes referred to as a salvation experience. When we experience a time and place in our lives that we know we are a sinner and we know that Jesus died for those sins, we can accept Him as our sin redemptor, our Lord and Savior because only He can clear us of our sinful nature. And just because we accept Him doesn't mean we will all of a sudden stop sinning. No, it means we are in the beginning stages of a relationship. This relationship, however, gives us the power to live in a sinful world today. And that's exactly the way we are to take it, Day by day, Oh dear Lord, three things I pray: To see thee more clearly, Love thee more dearly, Follow thee more nearly. Day by day. So true!

As shared in the Usefulness chapter, we are all being used to meet others' needs, and that is why it is so important to be connected with others—relationships. With our genetic family, our extended family, our church family, other groups that we are engaged in for many reasons, our colleagues, work teams, and the like.

Who comes to your support in times of need, and who do you support in their times of need?

In order to maintain a relationship at any level, we must invest some of our time into it. If we want that relationship to be strong, we must invest even more time. The time we are investing can be and should be exciting. Remember when you started dating your spouse or significant other? There was never enough time, and you did all sorts of things just to be together. The stories you shared about growing up or about college perhaps… In those sharing moments, you were not just passing time; you were growing roots in your relationship. And as you grew closer, the roots began to grow deeper, and every time you shared more about yourself, your roots became stronger. This is precisely the way your relationship with God develops. We first meet Him through some type of introduction, and then we accept Him as our salvation. He then becomes our friend and counselor.

We then began to spend more time together and share ourselves with Him. As we do this, we get closer and stronger, and our roots grow deeper, making our relationship stronger. God has given us a book that is explicit about the heart of God. He has literally put His heart on a shelf for us to take and read and grow closer to Him through it. Yes, it's the Holy Bible (God's Instructional Handbook for Life). But we don't have a book to give God, so we must talk to Him and express ourselves both verbally and emotionally through our ongoing relationship.

That means we can laugh, cry, sing, or express whatever we are feeling, and He understands us. The emotion that God has placed in His Bible is overwhelming at times. I used to think that my intense passionate side was a weakness. But I have come to learn that God is also passionate, and He has allowed us all to experience these feelings for many reasons. I have learned to count it as a blessing. As I interviewed many women for this book, we spent a great deal of time talking about relationships. What I most importantly learned was that most women shared patterns in their relationships. Their patterns showed that the way they managed their relationship with God was similar to the way they perceived or managed their relationships with others. What I found even more interesting is that although they agreed that their relationship with God was somehow on more of a higher level, there were patterns of feeling much closer at times, but that was typical to all of their relationships. If they described their relationship as a roller coaster, that meant that there were a lot of extreme up and down times of closeness (typically a trust issue). But even though they may not have been feeling so close at a time, they knew deep side that God was with them and that they were loved. I think this is a good illustration of the love of Christ. We don't always have to have that emotional high.

Like a husband or wife who can't be with their family for a day (or a week, month, etc.), but the love is still there. You don't take it away when you're not present for the day. It always exists. Although our emotions and passions are a gift from God, we must learn to reach deeper into our spirit and rely on the constants.

One woman shared with me that she was glad that God kept their relationship in the right perspective. When she fell away, He allowed things to happen in her life to draw her closer to Him, sometimes even closer than ever before. In retrospect, this seems too obvious. A loving God would not allow us to stray too far from home. He definitely speaks to us when we need it. This is how the relationship grows stronger. As we read in Hebrews 13:5, He will never leave us nor forsake us, and that makes this statement very personal.

I once worked with a gentleman who was going through a sensitively hard time during COVID-19, not because of COVID-19 but because his wife of twenty-five-plus years was fighting cancer, and her health was quickly declining. I do realize that COVID-19 was such a devastating time for the entire world, so much so that many of us were actually working from home with more flexible schedules. And God most certainly used this uncertainty in this gentleman's life to provide him with approximately seven hundred extra days at home with his wife prior to her passing. He worked from home and was available, so no lost time related to commuting, but they were able to eat lunch together every day; and he got to be there for her when it mattered the most. And as sad as this story ended for the two of them, he is now able to see that time as a true blessing. **PRAISE REPORT!** In their life and in their situation, this was a true gift from God.

There are other things in our lives that also influence our relationship with God, like the movies we watch. Have you ever watched the Hallmark Channel? My husband and I watch this periodically, and I have always been touched. There is one series of independent movies that I have seen on that channel where the story lines are all built on the good that occurs even in situations that appear to be not good (contrary to popular belief, not all of these shows are unrealistic). In the show I most remember, the main character was diagnosed with MS, and although that is something a person lives with throughout their life once diagnosed, there was a beautiful God Wink (expressions of joy) outcome.

This is reality—health issues, money problems, family confrontations...but I have adopted this God Wink reference in my own life as things change, some good and some more thought-provoking, but all are worthy of excitement, knowing that God has a plan and He will get me through it in His way and in His time. Anticipation maybe, but no worry.

As for Bible stories, these are real-life scenarios filled with heroes who demonstrate their personal relationship with God. King David is a great example—from slaying Goliath as a young boy to making seriously bad choices as a king. Even though he was chosen by God to be a leader, he wasn't perfect by any means. When as a king he chose sinful acts, he certainly paid for it royally (pun intended). And even though he fell, God never left him.

Thought: Look at your victories in the lens of God's working in your life as "supernatural."

Speaking of real-life heroes, it was a Monday night in a first-floor meeting room at the Holiday Inn. I liked this meeting room, as I had been there before for previous Mary Kay meetings. But this wasn't just any ordinary Monday meeting. Sitting there, I immediately noticed a new face in the group. She looked kind, but a little uneasy. Then she was introduced, and all I could see was her flashy red jacket with all the shiny pins she had earned and proudly displayed on each lapel. Awards I imagined, but how much does one need to accomplish to gain that assortment? I assumed she must know what she is doing to attain such a decorated attire. And although I wanted to introduce myself, I was suffering from a pretty aggravating migraine.

She returned the next Monday night meeting, and since I was feeling better, I was able to introduce myself to her. *Emma is "easygoing,"* I thought to myself—my kind of person. She was new to our group because she had relocated from another region and was invited to join our group for support. We started building a friendship on a professional level, and then as we spent more time, it became a more of a friendship. Emma offered to help me with my MK business, and after further conversations with me, she realized I really needed it! I didn't close properly, which wasn't helpful to the client or my business. Emma was truly a timely gift from God in more ways than one.

She took the time to work with me, which allowed me to become a top seller in my group. **PRAISE REPORT!**

As I write this chapter, I look over at my coffee mug filled with juice on this fine day. It reads, "Teamwork is the fuel that allows common people to perform uncommon results." What a statement to remember. With God on your team, you will be successful—a win-win situation regardless of the outcome because it is ordained by Him. You will produce uncommon results in all areas of your life as you grow closer and trust the living God that created you. Just the attitude adjustment is profound!

I have learned in my own personal situations that this foundational relationship with Jesus is vital to maintaining healthy relationships in all areas of my life. As we grow closer to Him, we are more equipped to be what He wants us to be, and this in return allows us to succeed at the relationships that are right for us. Relationships with our children, our parents, our spouses, our close friends, and coworkers— every relationship we have. Of course, some are significantly closer and stronger, but whichever, the important thing is that your relationship with God is right, and you can trust Him to help you maintain and cultivate all of your relationships. Healthy relationships are the key!

Generally, working through the pandemic was interesting to say the least. I was primarily working remotely with a few face-to-face interactions here and there. So about six months ago, I started looking in my hometown for a new house to be closer to my family because as I sit today, I am two and a half hours away from that city. I wanted to see them more regularly and spend more time with my young grandchildren.

To aid in the search, I was connected with a local realty agent, and she was helping me sort through the options. As you may have also learned, during this time, the housing market became quite inflated, as well as the interest rates. But it was worth exploring, so I continued to pray that God would lead us in the right direction and help us find something that we could modestly afford. Our agent was helpful and actually joined us at a few open houses in the area.

On one occasion, we looked at a home that had not yet been placed on the market because the owner's son was still preparing it to be formally listed, and we were invited to take a look at the house and share our thoughts, which the owner felt would help him to prepare for a sale overall. I really did like this home. It was an estate and had an amazing vintage vibe. The house itself was fairly up-to-date and in a nice neighborhood. When we arrived, I liked the house and totally appreciated the 1970s fully operating oven with pullout stove top. As we walked the house, I was amazed at all the decor that still remained; it was vintage and beautiful.

I mentioned early in our visit that if I were to purchase this property, I would ask the owner if I could also purchase this beautiful desk that flaunted the front picture window. It was unique and just appealed to me. This house would absolutely have been a great opportunity if it worked out, but after a full walk-through and discussion, my husband was not crazy about the property it sat on. I did totally understand his perspective because after living on a lake for six years, you would not have the same privacy there, and we knew we would have to invest a great deal more to create it. We did advise of our honest opinion that the home layout and appearance was fantastic; however, we were not personally interested due to the land it sat on, and that was something that could not be changed, so we thanked them and went our separate ways.

Shortly after, we received a call from our agent stating that the owner greatly appreciated our early feedback and wanted to give us a thank-you for taking the time to provide our unbiased opinion. Yes, he wanted to give me the desk that I had commented on that was in front of the picture window. I was seriously shocked, like when does that happen?

I am including this story because it is a perfect example of true generosity…something hard to find these days. I accepted the gift and made arrangements to pick it up. We met the owner on a Sunday afternoon, and he was just a fantastic person. When I looked at the desk again, I immediately knew that it would be the desk that I would write this book on—and I am. Needless to say, I am also grateful every day when I sit at this desk to share these stories. It makes me smile to know that something seemingly trivial to the naked eye would be such a huge impact on my mindset every day. God used

His generosity to provide the desk He wanted me to complete this book on. God is providing every little detail. **PRAISE REPORT!**

Before receiving this gift, I was using a four-foot folding table as my office desk. And yes, it would have worked out fine, but early that week, my son asked if I had a desk that I could give him to use at his recently purchased home, but at that time I did not. Obviously, when I received this desk, I immediately gave the other one to my son. TWO BLESSINGS occurred by one man's generosity. With that, I'm sending a huge shout out to both God for his provision and to Mr. Craig for his open and giving spirit. We should all be that unselfish. **PRAISE REPORT!**

As we venture on this road related to relationships, the following several stories shared are primarily from a group of women whom I had the amazing opportunity to interview many years ago. They shared how they were all uniquely introduced to Jesus and experienced faith in many different ways.

This first story was shared by Mary, a longtime friend of mine. Mary has truly been a blessing in my life…and not just because she potty-trained my oldest son.

She has been a faithful Christian for a long time and consistently seeks God and is confident that God hears her prayers and knows the desires of her heart. Her prayer life can be described as spontaneous and continuous conversation with Jesus.

Mary admits her Christian walk has been interesting. She had a full-out salvation experience and spent time getting closer to God and then backslid and then rededicated herself to Jesus. A little more about Mary: Inspiring music has a huge impact on her spirituality; she feels discontent when not in fellowship; is actively serving God and has throughout her life since experiencing her gift of salvation through serving in the children's ministry, being a van driver, and providing gifts to those in need.

But even though her relationship with God was so close and long-standing, even she got tripped up. The situation took place while entrenched in actively providing church-related support. She unexpectedly slipped into a relationship with a man who was not her husband, and it lasted for four months. She is ashamed that this happened but wants to share this story because she wants everyone to be aware that sin can creep into anyone's life at any time. It all seemed to happen so quickly, and when she realized she was living a double life, she was embarrassed and knew that she had hurt others.

This man was also a Christian, and they both became convicted and ended it. Immediately after they ended the inappropriate relationship, Mary went to her husband and confessed her sin in an attempt to reconcile. He was forgiving, but it was a painful experience for them both. She perceived his reaction and attitude toward learning of this situation as a huge intervention of God, as when he forgave her, she intensely felt the grace of God. She then sought counseling, realizing that she needed some other type of help since this happened. Through all of this, her marriage was restored and became even better than before. They experienced a greater level of communication throughout the process, have a stronger marriage, and are still together and loving the Lord after twenty years of this incident happening. **PRAISE REPORT!**

Not only did this experience humble her; it taught her to be more compassionate and understanding of others, as this is where she fell short in the past. She was admittedly judgmental and didn't understand or had trouble empathizing with others. It's no wonder that Mary's favorite Bible verse is 2 Corinthians 5:17: "If any man be in Christ, he is a new creature. Therefore, if anyone is in Christ, the new creation has come: The old has gone, the new is here!" I would add in this situation another great Bible verse that would closely apply. It is Isaiah 43:18: "Forget the former things; do not dwell on the past." MOVE FORWARD IN YOUR RELATIONSHIPS with others and with Jesus. We need to be made new and move forward. Get out the dump truck and dump the garbage out of your life.

LISTEN, evil is out there people, and it can impact anyone at any time. That is why it is so important to stay focused on the Lord. When attacked by the temptation of sin, don't let yourself be taken in; there is only negativity that comes as consequences. Yes, God can certainly use our shortcomings and make good of it, but the pain can be avoided. This is sometimes referred to as an attack, but God promises to never leave nor forsake us (Hebrews 13:5). So put on

His armor and prevail in Jesus Christ (Ephesians 6:16)—the armor of God: shield of faith, helmet of salvation and sword of the Spirit to resist the temptation of doing what you know is not edifying or appropriate. James 4:7 reads:

> Submit yourselves therefore to God. Resist
> the devil, and he will flee from you.

As an important mention, of the many women I have interviewed related to this book over many years, the most important commonality I found was that the prayer time was not a holy ritual per se; it is more like a daily ongoing conversation with God—more natural as if you were speaking with a friend, your best friend!

Another interesting finding was that these women also shared that although they had long-standing relationships with God, they felt that they had grown, as all relationships typically do, and their commitment had become stronger as they experience life with God's discernment.

One woman I interviewed shared that, to her, prayer life seemed like a battle, that things always popped up when she was trying to commit a particular time, and it turns out that she prays whenever and wherever. I know about this personally. I have actually prayed for parking spots, and most of the time, I get the one I need.

Another woman I met with shared a story about when she woke up in the middle of the night, intensely thinking about her son. She immediately gave it over to God in prayer and asked for God to help him without genuinely understanding why, and learned later that he was in a terrible snowstorm in an area that typically doesn't get snow. She could not have known that, nor did she need to identify the actual need at that moment, but she advocated for him and lifted him up in prayer, and God protected him.

That same woman shared a story with me about her hospitalization for meningitis and how she lifted the entire event up in prayer as she was experiencing it. She strangely had a peace that passed her own understanding throughout the experience although she was not sure what the outcome would be. It turned out that God used that situation to gather her husband and other family members who were at odds with each other to find a common ground and make amends. Through this situation, they found forgiveness.

Forgiveness is an amazing gift. Someone might hurt you, and you may rightfully choose to not be in their company, but choosing to forgive them is an entirely different decision. It's a way to personally influence the impact of their wrongdoing from negatively hurting you later down the road. It's a conscious decision. By not harboring ill will or unforgiveness, we can prevent added pain or illness in our own life, which typically leads to depression, clouded thinking, building a wall from prayer, relationship stress, physical illness, and the like. Forgive and you will be set free.

John 3:16 states, "For God so loved the world, that he gave his only Son, that whoever believes in him should not perish but have eternal life." Salvation is a relational experience—one that happens in a person's life and changes their thinking, changes their world. At the end of this book, you will have the opportunity to have your own salvation experience. Stay tuned!

An amazing story that is initially and specifically tied to a salvation experience and demonstrates God's tapestry begins with the funeral of Christina's grandmother. Being raised in a family where salvation was never shared, understood, or discussed, she had no clue what salvation truly was. But there was something different about this funeral service. The concept of salvation was shared.

Then a short time later in her life, her nephew was buried and again the same minister and the same message of salvation. These experiences were Christina's only exposure to salvation at this point in her lifetime. But looking back later in life, it is so obvious to see these were clearly stepping stones that God had placed in her life to lead her down the right path.

In 1987, Christina sensed something was wrong as she walked down the hall and saw her father lying on the floor. Her mother was crying hysterically above his pale, still body. She saw her siblings' facial expressions of despair. Her father had died. His heart had stopped. He was just motionlessly lying there on the floor of their home, and just then, the paramedics arrived and performed CPR. Miraculously, they revived him.

As the family did not know at that time, God planned another miracle through this incident. It was a tiny prayer that her father had prayed the evening before his encounter with death. In a drunken stupor, he prayed, "Help me, Lord, to be a new man, a better person. I can't do it alone. It's out of my control." This heartfelt prayer came from a desperate and out-of-control man who wasn't even sure if God was listening to him. But God did hear him, and in fact, God answered him by allowing him to almost lose the very thing he took for granted—his life. **PRAISE REPORT!**

After being seen by doctors and learning of this newly found heart condition, Mike was sworn off alcohol and cigarettes—his two favorite pastimes. This was the beginning of a new Journey for the entire family. Now that he was homebound and most of his abusive influences were gone, the many long nights and horrible fights between her mother and father had finally stopped. A long hospital stay and many lifestyle changes were just the initial events that led to a closer-knit family. They each now had a newly found respect for life and for each other. Mike was now pressed to relinquish his rough, tough, controlling attitudes that he thought was what made a real man because now, for the first time in his life, he was fully dependent on his wife for everything.

Five years later, Christina met Chad. Chad was a different kind of man from her overall perception of men. He was actually a nice guy and, as she added, an exceptionally good-looking guy at that. But there was something more intriguing about him than his niceness and his good looks. This guy had another special attribute, and she was soon to learn it was his faith in Jesus—a strong faith and a relationship with God. To Christina, it gave him a certain kind of glow and separated him from any other guy she had met in the past. After initially meeting him, they went their own ways in the natural course of life, and then after several months, she wanted to see him again, but this time to perhaps to make a date, so she stepped out in faith and gave him a call. After a longer than expected conversation over the phone, they learned that they both felt the same attraction, and a more interesting relationship began to bud. By Christmas that year, they were dating exclusively.

Then on Valentine's Day, Chad shared with her the way to her own personal relationship with Jesus as one of his special gifts to her. How sweet is that? After contemplating what he had shared throughout the rest of that evening, she later woke in tears, asking Jesus into her heart. She knew that she needed His strength, direction, and wisdom and poured out her heart to God. Before she fell back to sleep, she had an overwhelming sense of being embraced by God, and her heavy load was uplifted—a truly life-changing moment. All of her past experiences had primed her heart for this instance, and with this new passion and energy, she was on a mission, a mission to share that same gift that was given to her with her family that she loved so very much. Although at this time they weren't as moved, but they respected her decision.

Christina soon found a local Bible-believing and God-loving church to attend. When she first went there, the first thing she noticed was that the pastor's face was strangely familiar. And as she contemplated why that was, she ironically realized that it was the same man that buried her grandmother and nephew years before— the pastor who shared her first exposure to the gift of salvation.

As she began to attend this church more regularly, she learned for herself that the church was a place to help her to grow closer to God through continually hearing Spirit-inspired messages and encouragement to stay connected to God, and to engage with other like-minded Christians and experience uplifting fellowship. She wanted her family to have this same experience and continually invited her family to accompany her.

Approximately two years later, on a beautiful spring day, Christina was finally successful in convincing her dad to attend with her, and what a perfect timing. He needed to hear that message that was shared that morning, and he accepted Jesus in that service. This was yet another huge stepping stone in their lives. Her mother, sister, and brother soon followed his lead, and the joy overwhelmed them. It was like their eyes were now open to see that God's hand had been in their lives so directly and precisely, even back when life was so different.

After this event, Mike's attitude and sensitivity was being developed by God, and he looked for things to show God's hand moving in his life. A couple years later, he experienced a stroke but saw it as God's way of teaching him the proper way to use his speech because for twenty-five minutes, he couldn't talk. There again, another example of looking for the good and positive in all of life's situations—even the hard ones. God has kept His hand on this family as He does for all who ask. This family was not exempt from the so-called bad experiences of life but have instead learned to look for and see the good in all of it and truly embrace the good.

Sometimes God answers our prayers in ways we could never imagine. It could take a devastating event to open our eyes. And aligned to the premise of this book, God uses seemingly bad situations to make amazing things happen to bring blessings in the midst of the storm. **PRAISE REPORT!**

This is when we need not fear and let God have the reins and control, but it is certainly one of the hardest things to do. Most of the stories in this book share a similar theme, that when we learn to keep our focus on God and share our thankfulness, it makes life somewhat easier and more meaningful. *In His time*, He turns the situation into a blessing, and that's the best anyone could ask for. And His answers are not always what we imagine them to be, but that's part of the joy and excitement, just recognizing them and knowing they are a gift regardless—a gift meant ultimately for our good.

Imagine being used by the Almighty God to bring a miracle into someone else's life. What could be more fulfilling?

When I asked Christina about her prayer pattern, thinking she would say she dedicated a certain amount of time each day to spend with the Lord, I was wrong. She prays in the shower, she prays driving to work, she prays all day long. And like mentioned prior, it is a relationship, not just a particular time set aside. Spending time with God was an all-day experience, and not an event, although almost every evening, she and her husband do pray together. That is a special time for her because together they humble themselves before God and each other.

Another part of Christina's tapestry that must be shared is that she and Chad met as virgins and committed themselves to each other as gifts for each other from God. I know this is a bit personal, but their relationship with God has enhanced their relationship with each other as they accepted themselves as a gift from God and attempt daily to treat each other accordingly. Christina had shared with me one year after their marriage that as they both continually foster their relationship with God, it enhances their attitudes and strength of their friendship, knowing that God's love is not a one-time occurrence or event; it's a relationship that's an ongoing, lifetime experience. **PRAISE REPORT!**

To preface this next testimony that includes two miracles, it is important to know that Melony describes herself as a strong-willed, controlling, and assertive personality type. She feels strongly that this is because she is trying to own her part in this world, but God stopped her in her tracks at a time and place that eventually impacted her life forever, in a way that caused her to listen and learn from Him, instead of kicking Him out of her life when things got tough because that was her way in all relationships. She would later experience and accept His amazing love and support for her.

Her story begins primarily around her fairy-tale marriage. Then life happens…accumulated failures and a lack of a deeper spiritual connection versus primarily physical attraction caused overall withdrawal from her relationship. This disconnect was soon after enhanced by a poor emotional state after another traumatic life happening. Consequently, her husband opened himself up to another woman…a woman with no baggage and no known knowledge of his baggage. It's not a game show, folks; it's real life. These things unfortunately happen every day.

Her husband's betrayal left her devastated and even more alienated due to lack of love and support. To Melony, he was her closest friend and bond in this world, and now that was broken. He soon moved out of their home once they were faced with the reality that his secret was out, but that was what she needed to personally face the reality of the situation. In the pain of this happening, she knew that no human could help her; she was crushed.

His removal from their home lasted a year, so this realization and healing process did not happen overnight. She was not in a forgiving state. They had children and still had to somewhat regularly engage; therefore, the confrontations still occurred, but more irregularly than when he was there at the home twenty-four seven. Then one day, while Melony was in deep prayer, God revealed to her that this void could only be filled by God and His unconditional love, which is deeper and sustaining, no matter what the outcome.

Her husband was also going through his own personal trauma at the time. His grief and anger over losing his mother and then the devastation of their brother's suicide experience brought the entire family to their knees. And over time, this closer walk with God had restored the family's relationships by inducing personal growth and transparency and, ultimately, a stronger relationship with God. **PRAISE REPORT!**

Seriously, know that people are hurting out there; everything is not just about YOU.

Truth be told, they both needed professional counseling for everything they had been through, but unfortunately, his insurance would not cover it. As Melony describes the miracle in this situation, it was when she called her insurance company, described the situation, and due to the severity of his need, the insurance company agreed to let him get counseling under her policy. Well, we all know this is NOT a typical outcome when dealing with an insurance company, but God made it happen! **PRAISE REPORT!**

This entire situation led her into the arms of Jesus. He was now her safe haven. Knowing she had her own shortcomings made it easier to understand, but she was now forced to rely on God's Scripture and the Holy Spirit's leading versus herself as in the past. She closed our interview by sharing that "no man's wisdom can compare to God's." The importance of forgiveness is a true freedom for all parties impacted, and transparency and openness are the keys. *NO ONE IS PERFECT.*

And true humility—it is a gift. Have you ever started to feel prideful, and then something weird happens, like you hit your own head with the car door when entering the car? That's what happened to me once, and I will never forget it. Yes, something that strange is what keeps me humble.

Melony and her husband are now amazingly close, closer than ever, and they pray together on many occasions. Their newly restored relationship is closer, more authentic, and trusting. God carried her through this time and allowed her to withdraw from the negative actions that result from the infidelity. She had to focus on getting stronger internally by relying on God solely. **PRAISE REPORT!**

Today, she would tell you she has been BLESSED by this entire situation because otherwise, her relationship with her husband would not be on this same incredible level. She would also admit that being so busy in her own life, she missed a lot of signals and warning signs. This situation also taught her to stop looking and stop running from her insecurities.

REFLECTION: James 5:16 reads: "Confess your faults and pray for one another, that you may be healed. The effectual fervent prayer of a righteous man avails much."

Melony has experienced for herself how God can take the wrong choices made in our past and turn them into blessings beyond our wildest dreams. She reflected on what could have happened and is even more thankful that her children were able to grow up with their father and that they have all learned a great deal through these experiences and have all now found a relationship with God themselves. Every seemingly tragic situation we experience is an opportunity to grow and refine our intentions. And she shared that God isn't done with her yet. She looks forward to experiencing God in all areas of her life. Melony has used these life learning experiences to help grow and support others, especially those going through difficult emotional times. She leads them to God's Word and promises and shares her journal poetry.

As often heard and quoted by Homer, "I don't know what the future holds, but I know who holds the future." What a comfort this statement is. But to add, I can't help but mention what my pastor has always shared, and I am paraphrasing, "Work like it's in your hands, and pray for direction knowing it is in God's hands." I refer to this as the Tapestry of Life, how God allows the intertwined events and circumstances in our lives to create His purpose—just like recycling, turning seemingly leftover material into tangible, useful, and valuable things. **PRAISE REPORT!**

Who is leading and directing your tapestry, your legacy?

Melony also wanted to share a little about her salvation experience, as early in her exposure and introduction to Jesus, she could have been described as a "Jesus freak" because she was so emotionally elated. That was her initial and purely emotional reaction. Her experience was based on not having a more in-depth knowledge and experience in God's Word nor any real nurturing. Her sentiment reaffirms our need to get into God's Word in the many ways available like Bible studies, church sermons, prayer groups, daily reflection resources, Bible promises books, and the like.

What it comes down to is that if we haven't experienced both good and bad situations in our own lives, how can we provide empathic support for others? These experiences make us better equipped, just like your work experiences make you better and more well equipped. And Praise God that we don't live cookie-cutter lives.

God's hand is directly impacting our world, including the people He allows us to meet. Whether we are helping them, or they are helping us, it's an amazing tapestry. After all of her experiences, both good and challenging, Melony's favorite Bible verse is "I can do all things through Christ who Strengthens me" (Philippians 4:13).

As a sidenote, I was once referred to as a Jesus freak, and I took it as the ultimate compliment, and now being more mature in my relationship, I still would!

Another story I want to share is from one of my friends, and although I have already introduced her in this book, this is her story. I met Emma at a Mary Kay meeting, and she was a great influence in my career. God used her to help me in a time of need.

During her interview, Emma agreed that her relationship with God was like a roller coaster, as it is for many of us, and correlated directly with her earthly relationships. She was trying to read the Bible, attend church services to fellowship with others of faith and to grow closer in her spiritual Journey, and ultimately make better God-led choices. She also shared that her prayer life was also sporadic and a throughout-the-day activity, which is consistent to most of the women I interviewed, including myself.

Her interpretation of a miracle was the God connection in divine intervention, and she admitted that she had experienced miracles in her lifetime, especially when she was in college and was under a great deal of pressure. She met her soon-to-be husband at college, and he was truly godsent. They later moved out of state to Missouri after a great deal of prayer about the decision. It was a tough decision primarily because it required her to move away from her family and friends, but she approached it prayerfully and felt God's peace with her decision, and eventually, they made the move. And even though after the move she felt alienated, she also felt closer to God for that reason and counted that as a blessing.

Now in their "new" hometown, she was given the opportunity to witness her relationship to God with a Jewish friend. He was hospitalized, and she was there for him and prayed for him. Trying times are sad and hard, but also some of the best opportunities to be a true friend—to be there for that person and show them God's love. After all, we are an extension of God's love. "We are His heartbeat in our own communities." **PRAISE REPORT!**

This story reminds me of a time when my oldest son was hospitalized. It was in the winter months and was a cold and snowy season at that. As an adult at this time, he called to tell me he was being admitted into the hospital for testing, as the doctors were not sure what was wrong with him. (Later, they learned it was gall stones) I wanted to be there for him, so my husband and I drove out to the hospital, which was a bit of a distance. It took three times the travel time due to the inclement weather conditions. I share this to accentuate the intensity of the storm.

When we arrived, he had a friend there with him, a roommate of his whom I had never met before. Her name was Ana. After a quick introduction, we discovered that Ana WALKED several miles in that cold, blistering weather to bring my son needed clothes for his hospital stay. From that day on, I just loved this woman. I was just so touched that she did this for a friend in need. She was not a Christian at the time, but what a powerful example of "showing love to your neighbor." Sure, it's easy to bake a pie or dish and take it over or send something via mail, and these are all important things, but her act was extraordinary. And at that time, they were just friends, and for a long time after.

The most wonderful thing that happened in this friendship in my opinion is that many years later, that relationship eventually grew, and they are now happily married and sharing their love for Jesus together—two very committed individuals who are growing in God's love and sharing God's Word and witnessing their experiences daily. **PRAISE REPORT!**

My next shared story is with Laureen. Laureen was another business colleague of mine and later friend whom I met through the Mary Kay company. She was a successful sales manager and role model and mentored many women to be successful as well. And although Laureen experienced her salvation experience at a young age at her church youth group, it took many years for her to learn the true power of God.

Her prayer time is inconsistent, and she doesn't make a daily ritual of it, as it is more of a conversation with God throughout the day. Reading inspirational writings including the Bible help her grow and stay closer to God as well.

And Laureen is not shy about sharing her love of God with others. She actually uses her job as an opportunity to minister to other women. She has learned over many years that God has given us all gifts; sometimes they are similar and sometimes different, but always when and where we need them. The important thing is that we need to allow the Spirit to lead us and not make it of our own prideful selves. Yes, we all have that tendency in different situations, and I'm sure God can find a way to use that as well.

It's about growing and maturing in our relationship with Christ as God provides us direction, speaks to our heart, and demonstrates miracles, and He does these things every day throughout different challenges in our lives. Her advice is to keep growing, find openness in praying and talking to God daily to support your personal relationship and decisions that need to be made. She calls this "walking with God." She would add that journaling her experiences help too!

To further add to the concept of prayer and praise journaling, consider the message in Philippians 4:6: "Do not be anxious about anything, but in everything by prayer and supplication with thanksgiving let your requests be made known to God." We really need to come together and share in a time of praise and thanksgiving, lifting our requests to God. This is where prayer and praise journaling is helpful. It not only allows us to keep track of our answered prayers but also to remind us of God constantly moving in our lives. God answers prayers; I can attest to it as well as the women who graciously shared their stories for this book, but it will always be in His perfect time—the power of a thankful heart.

RECOMMENDATION: Create your own Prayer and Praise box: Take an old shoe box, cut a slot on the top, cover it with uplifting wrapping paper, and begin to write your prayers and praises daily and put them in the box. It's an amazing way to document your communication with God, especially if you're a writer. ☺

One major life event that Laureen experienced as a committed Christian is when her husband was diagnosed with prostate cancer. They sought out the best care possible, which took them to a hospital in the state of Indiana. Going into the trip, she referred to it as their "Miracle Road Trip," and it ended up being exactly just that. Not only did her husband get the medical care and attention he needed when he needed it, but Laureen was his support throughout. She was already blessed to be in a flexible job situation, and therefore, was able to take the trip with him. And although this was a scary and unsmooth road that they had never been down before, it was definitely a tool that God used to allow them to spend time together, to become closer with each other and closer with God as a couple.

God doesn't make bad things happen to us; it's just the nature of being on earth—exposure to things out of our control or even consequences perhaps of decisions we've made along the way—but the beauty is that He can use these conditions to mold us into the person we need to become to be happier, more satisfied, and more helpful to others.

There were other ways that God took care of them through this cancer experience including interesting connections of support like the hospital doctors engaged, the impact this situation made on their teenage children that was used to help them to not fear death, having a sense of taking Spirit-led control and just dealing with problems in general because none of us are exempt from problems in this life.

Throughout this situation, Laureen felt a sense of God's presence above any other time in her life. She felt that when she was speaking with a doctor, or a nurse, or anyone about the situation, she knew God's presence was with her. She mentioned it in this manner: "When you think there is two, you know there is three." And this situation was in no way easy for either of them, but it was almost like an adventure where they kept looking for God's intervention and were elated and praised Him when they were blessed to see it. They also learned that it is in God's strength, not theirs, that they got through this situation and every other life situation. To top it off, Laureen's husband was healed from this cancer through this engagement and is in full remission. **PRAISE REPORT!**

Laureen's favorite Bible verse is Psalm 27:1, "The LORD is my light and my salvation; whom shall I fear? The LORD is the strength of my life; of whom shall I be afraid?" She internalizes this verse as a reminder to not be afraid when faced with hard situations because God's hand is fully in control of her life.

As another testimony, I once knew a great lady who was actually one of the five adult witnesses at my third wedding. We'll call her Sherry. Not only did Sherry attend my wedding; she surprised us and sang a beautiful song that made the occasion even more special. This woman admits that she met God by watching an evangelist on TV. It was at a time in her life when she was having a great deal of problems and heard a message that God could help her. Yes, she is a self-proclaimed extremist, and this opportunity was taken to the extreme, but she immediately sought out a Bible-preaching church in her area to help her grow in the Lord.

She shared with me that her past relationships were not consistent, not even with her own father, as they had not spoken for over eighteen years. But later in life, as she grew closer to God and learned about His love and forgiveness, they did find a way to make amends. **PRAISE REPORT!** But she agrees that the pride and stubbornness of both parties accounted for missing a great deal of each other's lives. And although the relationship is something that can be restored, the time lost cannot be recreated.

And through this experience, she personally recognizes that FORGIVENESS is an amazing tool and that it heals both parties. Sometimes a person is not healthy for us to be around, but learning to forgive is the important element and then make those decisions moving forward as to who you spend your time with. When you spend time with God, asking for His direction, you will know where and with whom you need to be.

It's also about humility. You need to find a way to stay humble, or God will allow you to be humbled. Remember the experience I shared about the car door? You don't want to experience that or possibly something worse.

As mentioned, this woman is a musician, and what a beautiful voice she is gifted with. She is our favorite church singer, but she wasn't always a singer as she experienced a miracle earlier in her life. Many years prior, she had a hearing problem, and after many doctor consults and medical tests, she was finally convinced that only a surgery would fix the underlying issue; but she was not happy about it and did not want to face surgery. Then after much prayer, she agreed to have the surgery, and it ended up being exactly what she needed to face to become the beautiful artist she is today.

In her life, this was a true miracle. God uses our medical teams as much as He uses others in our lives to perform His will. She would not have had the opportunity to share the beautiful gift of her voice with others had she not stepped out in faith and had the surgery she desperately needed. It was life-changing.

Initially, she began singing at a local club as part of a trio and learned a great deal through that experience. And then later in her life, when finding a fitting church to praise God and be edified, she was able to demonstrate that gift and talent as a blessing to bless others. I am a witness! When she started attending this church, she just felt God's Spirit and knew that's where she needed to be. Her relationship with God has only strengthened, and she is a true witness to "hearing" God's voice and following it to receive her healing miracle that positively changed her life.

Her favorite Bible verse is Psalm 23:1–6 because it gives her a sense of peace when facing fearful times.

> The LORD is my shepherd; I shall not want,
> He maketh me to lie down in green pastures: he leadeth me beside the still waters. He restoreth my soul: he leadeth me in the paths of righteousness for his name's sake. Yea, though I walk through the valley of the shadow of death, I will fear no evil: for thou art with me; thy rod and thy staff they comfort me. Thou preparest a table before me in the presence of mine enemies: thou anointest my head with oil; my cup runneth over. Surely goodness and mercy shall follow me all the days of my life: and I will dwell in the house of the LORD forever.

Additionally, she is thankful for everything, even for challenges and daily battles, because not only does it draw her closer to God; it keeps her in God's will, and to her that is where the comfort in times of storms comes from.

Now, I'd like to introduce you to Susan. Susan is a woman who refers to her relationship with God now as committed and consistently close. She described her salvation experience many years prior to our interview as a time when she was at a low point in her life, as she had just experienced a broken marriage engagement and felt that the world was going to end due to the pain of betrayal—the hurt and anger that resulted emotionally.

As she matured in her relationship with God, she realized that the incident was actually a blessing in disguise. Her life now is especially different. She sees life and her relationship with God as a continuous learning process. "Having zeal without knowledge"—THAT is a powerful expression and not an easy thing to do. Usually, it takes these types of past experiences to reflect back on to learn how to trust.

She now feels that she is close to God as a choice to listen to Him and make faith-based decisions tied to His speaking to her heart, a choice, like many others we make in our lives, to commune with God regularly and to let His power work in our lives in many ways. This is a woman who literally prays throughout the day. She prays in the car; between jobs; sometimes at her job; if and when possible, her drive back home; and prior to heading to bed for the night.

One situation she shared that was close to her heart was her parents' salvation story. They happened on two different occasions but were most definitely a result of answered prayers. Her father experienced a medical condition that caused his heart to beat irregularly and actually stopping at times. When he had to address this with pacemaker surgery, she believes it was at that time when he became vulnerable to realizing we only have one go at this life, and he wanted to make it better.

And as for her mother, she had her own bout with breast cancer, and as you can either imagine or have experienced yourself, this is also a life-changing diagnosis. Just dealing with the treatment and other issues gives a person a lot of time to think and contemplate their life and legacy. And as an additional twist to this praise story, Susan had just returned from a job out of state that allowed her to be there for her parents during this hard time. God's timing is always perfect. **PRAISE REPORT!**

These were the situations that brought her parents to Christ, and although they are scary earthly situations, she is grateful that they resulted in her parents meeting God, trusting God, and eventually experiencing eternal life in heaven when God calls them home. That is a true blessing, knowing that your loved ones will spend eternity with our loving God, especially when a few years after her father found the power of Jesus in his life, he began to experience Alzheimer's symptoms. So yes, his time of mental recognition was limited.

These were two huge miracles in Susan's life, as her definition of a miracle is a supernatural movement—when all things align in a perfect way even in imperfect situations. It's no wonder that Susan's favorite Bible verse is Romans 8:28, "And we know that all things work together for good to them that love God, to them who are the called according to his purpose." It is aligned to the very essence why I am writing this book! **PRAISE REPORT!**

Nobody's perfect, but only through Jesus are we forgiven!

For this next interview, I never actually met this interesting woman face-to-face, and to keep her confidentiality, I will refer to her as Amy. I did, however, meet her husband on an airplane. He's the gentleman who gave me the reality check that God was flying the plane, and since that engagement, I have never feared flying and have actually learned to embrace the opportunity and "enjoy each Journey" as well. After sharing the book concept with him during that encounter, he introduced me to his wife over the phone. This is Amy's story and inspiration.

Having been raised Catholic, she believed she never had an actual salvation experience, although she knew she needed to have a more personal relationship with Christ. She attended CCD classes and learned to pray, as well as partaking in the many traditions of Catholicism, but what really stuck with her was learning about the Bible and the stories of God's faithfulness.

She admits that her parents were not the best Christian role model; her father rarely attended church, and her mother was a perfect example of what Amy calls the "hit-and-run philosophy." She attended out of duty and not for her love of the Lord. Her father was an alcoholic, and her parents ended up getting a divorce when she was in seventh grade. I share this because it is a testament that we all have different paths in life, at every stage of life to boot.

She remembers that she was taught to pray, but what she wasn't sure of until she matured later in life was that God answers prayers, maybe just not in the way we ask for them to be answered. She had learned "it is His way, not ours." She learned this as a child when she prayed that her parents would not get a divorce, but her prayers were not answered the way she wanted but later learned that it was definitely for the best in that particular situation. She recalls being upset with God for allowing that to happen...for "sending her dad away." But she knows now that it was her father's choice, not God's.

With that upbringing, along with a diagnosis of multiple sclerosis (MS) in her early twenties and the listless church experience she suffered through as a youth, she tried to understand and appreciate more each day what the gift of salvation meant to her. Especially during the time when she had the MS diagnosis, she questioned her faith altogether.

Years later, after meeting her now-husband Tom, growing together, and seeking God's influence together, they sought to know God in a more intimate way. They began attending different churches to find a true fellowship experience but didn't feel welcomed in any of them. (Seriously, what a shame.)

Then after the birth of their first child, they found a church that truly WELCOMED THEM, and they were uplifted. This church spoke of Jesus with great joy and seemed to demonstrate the peace that you read about in the Bible…the peace that passes all understanding. Philippians 4:7 reads, "And the peace of God which passeth all understanding, shall keep your hearts and minds through Christ Jesus." And thus began their spiritual Journey together.

Amy decided to attend a nondenominational women's Bible study at the church. It was called "A Women's Heart, God's Dwelling Place" and was a study of the Old Testament, and she agreed it was phenomenal. And although she learned a great deal and made some fantastic connections, it made her question why she had not learned of this amazing gift from God earlier in her life in her so-called Christian walk. She left this experience, enthusiastic to learn more and share her love of God, as well as making some great connections, which later turned into friendships. SO POWERFUL. **PRAISE REPORT!**

In raising their children, Amy knew she needed God's help to be a good mom, to have discernment in making decisions—like the language and attitudes she reflected—by inspiring her family by making changes such as watching more wholesome movies. She even took it to the level of how she decorated her home to put more focus on the positive and reflections of her relationship with God.

Amy felt the desire to share her story with others when she felt God's prompting. She admitted that it is a daily commitment and recognizes how she can rely on God to show her the way. She wants to live each day as Jesus would have her live. She monitors her children's exposure to the "unholy" even if it's the opposite of what their friends and family are doing. Sometimes it's hard, she admits, but she knows that her family's individual relationship with God is the most important. She tries at every opportunity to edify herself with Christian influences, especially when it comes to the radio, TV, and Internet. This was a decision for her and her husband—to bring their children up knowing God, as well as fostering a relationship with God.

Amy has even been accused by her own mother as "brainwashing" her kids because of her commitment to God, but she tells it like it is. You're either brainwashing them with the world and its influences without your control, or you are brainwashing them with more wholesome things and to know and aspire to have a relationship with Jesus. This is a powerful statement. **PRAISE REPORT!**

She gets excited when her oldest son skips around the house singing, "Our God is an awesome God" versus what she calls potential junk they can pick up off the radio. And even though she makes these thoughtful decisions for her family, she admits that her relationship with God is like a roller coaster. She has her up and down times, and her prayer time is not a set time each day; it's on an as-needed basis or as inspired throughout the day—again, aligned with the many others I have interviewed—and she praises God each moment of each day as she sees the beauty He has brought into her life.

Amy admits that her relationship with God has been interesting. She experienced times of drifting away slowly until she recognized she needs His inspiration. And her Journey is not always smooth, as she knows what she needs to do but has trouble putting it into action when things get extremely busy. But that's where it becomes more interesting. She realizes that she has to make time to stay close to God, to read His Word, to pray, and to fellowship when viable. I get it; we all live busy lives, and making time to be with God can get put on the sidelines. The beauty of God's Bible promises is that He will never leave you nor forsake you. In those times and always, it's never about what WE can DO; it's about where our heart is and to stay open to Jesus so He can use us in His great wisdom.

Amy prefers to surround herself with like-minded people, so she and her husband have made friends with other Christians living their Journey with a relationship with Jesus. It helps them to stay on track. She also has a sense of discernment that I admire. She knows that not every thought that comes across her mind is Spirit-led, and sometimes maybe the opposite; therefore, her fervent daily prayer is to know the difference and act on God's prompting, which is always for the good because GOD IS GOOD!

Another thing I admire is that she strives to set an example for her children by her chosen lifestyle, but without being overbearing. She prays with her children at mealtime to teach them to be grateful, for everything comes from God. She prays with them at night to comfort and help them to rest, knowing God's protection is on them. This is not a learned behavior passed down through her family; this is a conscious effort on her part to teach her children and to be a parental mentor.

When I asked about her experience with miracles in her lifetime, this is the first thing she responded with: "I am not sure what a miracle means to others, but to me, I look at miracles every day when I look at my three children…just to think how they each started life and grew from two united cells into wonderfully detailed humans, from the smallest eyelash to the intricacy of their brain-organ relationship. I just don't see how anyone could not see God's hand in the making of each new life." How truly powerful is that statement? **PRAISE REPORT**!

Another captivating callout that Amy made was related to her prayer life. She said that sometimes God says "No," and although it is always for our own good, it is hard to understand at times. This is where she quoted James 1:2, a verse that was shared with her by a family friend that states, "Count it all Joy when faced with trials of many kinds!" This has encouraged her to try to step back from a bad situation and seriously look for the good; it's always there somewhere…and as a reminder that God is ultimately in control, and if and when trials arise, there is a reason for it. Usually that reason is far beyond what we can see at the time. She has struggled with this but is now choosing to avoid the PMS (Poor Me Syndrome) that she had taken on in the past. **PRAISE REPORT!**

Amy credits reading the Bible and attending Bible studies as a huge support in her spiritual Journey. Learning of God's promises and reading about His biblical miracles are inspirational for her. Jesus certainly died on that cross for all of us. We are all sinners, and no one is perfect. I'm personally grateful that the pressure is off, and I can enjoy the Journey that God has set before me with an excitement in my heart, just thinking about what He has for me next!

Another idea I want to share from Amy is that although she is a committed Christian, she realizes that struggles are a part of life and no one is exempt, but how much more comforting it is to know you have God's support? No one is guaranteed a rosy life, not even by being a Christian. It's the nature of this world and the negativity we experience in this world. Furthermore, she has actually learned that it is on the contrary; you can face even more trials because of your beliefs. Sometimes your Journey faces more struggles as you set your heart on doing God's will. She once saw a sign that stated, "the road to success is always under construction," and she was touched by it, tied to her relationship with God. Thank you, Amy. I personally LOVE IT, as it aligns with my walk with God as well.

It's no surprise, by her testimony, that Amy's favorite Bible verse is Joshua 24:15, "As for me and my house, we will serve the Lord." Her thoughts behind choosing this verse of all the other great verses from the Bible is that it is a reminder to her to make a conscious choice each day to serve God and encourages her to continue to find out how. This is her personal goal, to understand how she can best serve the Lord and to pass that on to her children. This will surely be her legacy. **PRAISE REPORT!**

God certainly has a way of dealing with each one of us in His own special way. There is a tapestry or interwoven series of events that occur to expose us to God's reality if we choose to look for these events and situations. Our spiritual eyes will be more open to see them, and although we can't always see them on the front end, later on down the road, we can later see the big picture. Looking back in retrospect, sometimes we can see it unfold before our very eyes if God ordains for us to see it. PRAY FOR VISION.

When we go into situations looking for the good or the positive, it becomes much clearer to see it. But if we look for or expect bad things and take it at face value, it can and will pull you down into negativity. Try this exercise on any certain day that you're out and about. Choose a color and think on it. You will quickly see that your world becomes full of that color—it's everywhere. Now try this same exercise with a particular make of car, perhaps a Jeep Grand Cherokee (my favorite) or anything you favor. You will discover that there are many all around you, although you didn't notice them much until you made a conscious effort to. This is how the principle of finding the good in everything works. What you consciously or intently look for, you will find. I personally believe and have witnessed how God has allowed good to come from all situations. If you are reading this book, know that "all things work together for good for those who love the Lord, those who are called according to his purpose" (Romans 8:28).

Chapter N = Needs (Ours and Others)

✦

I interviewed a church friend years back. Her name is Crystal. Crystal's mantra was that "strength is from God; His support is from others." This coming from a person who experienced her salvation at the age of eight years old. See, Crystal was adopted by a loving family as a child, after years of foster care. She learned later in life the profile of her biological family: Her father was imprisoned, her mother was unknown, and she had two sisters. She firmly believes that adoption saved her and her sisters from sexual abuse exposure. She became closer to God as a teen and still appreciates how her life was spared. She claims this Bible verse, Jeremiah 29:11: "For I know the plans I have for you, declares the LORD, plans to prosper you and not to harm you, to give you a future and a hope." **PRAISE REPORT!**

> The Lord is my light and my salvation,
> whom shall I fear? (Psalm 27:1)

When it comes to meeting needs, not everything is so front and center when it is received. But I have an interesting story about a simple book that was shared with me years back. The book is entitled *I Believe in You* by Sandy Gingras.

It was given to me by a coworker as a birthday gift years back. And although I greatly appreciated it when it was received, I greatly appreciated it so much more just recently when my job was impacted by a COVID-19 restructuring, and my position was eliminated. I was cleaning my home-office desk and stumbled upon it. I read it again, and it touched my heart. It was so meaningful and inspirational, especially because it was the first time in my career that I experienced this type of professional separation. In the past, it was always by my decision.

This little book has a great deal of meaning for me at this time, and for that I am grateful, so grateful that I reached out to the Spirit-led giver to make sure she was aware of the positive impact it had made on me even now, years after the gift was given. **PRAISE REPORT!** (Thank you, Marily!)

FOLLOW GOD'S PROMPTING, as it might be for a future need!

Meeting other people's needs is a true blessing. Have you ever had the chance to totally out of the blue just help someone?

In the Usefulness chapter, I shared the story about my opportunity to make another person's holiday a blessing. And although it was a collective effort to make it happen, it brought me great joy to be able to coordinate the gift and knowing I was in God's will for her.

What can you do today to make another person's life feel special and cared for, especially if they are in a time of need?

When I was pregnant with my third son, several weeks prior to delivery, my doctor ordered me on bed rest because of the swelling in my legs and feet. It was tough being on bed rest and taking care of a seven-year-old and a two-year-old, but my oldest son was truly an amazing blessing. Thank God he was old enough to be a "helper"!

But in speaking of meeting needs, think about not being able to get up and cook meals for your kids. That was time when we didn't have UBER Eats and home delivery. Furthermore, I was still kind of struggling financially. But God come through to my rescue. He used the help and loving support of my church family to make it happen. They came to my home with a prepared hot meal, and sometimes a great dessert too, every day for those weeks until my son was born. It is hard to put in words how that impacted my life at that moment as well as even now, thirty years after. It was a HUGE BLESSING that I know was God-inspired. People gave up their time and resources to care for me and my children in a time of need. **PRAISE REPORT!**

"In all Things, Give Thanks," (1 Thessalonians 5:18). This is gratefulness.

As I mentioned early in the book, as the author, I absolutely can identify with almost everyone out there. I am by no means perfect or holier than thou. I have my own struggles and a not-so-perfect past. And as I have also mentioned, part of that not-so-perfect past includes two failed marriages. But even though the marriages failed, God did not fail me. As a result of those situations, I have two amazing sons to show for them.

My older son was born in a situation where I was young, and I always say that he helped me grow up, and since I was still young when I had my second son, he had a good hand in learning with me as well. (So thank you to my two oldest baby boys. You have always been amazing friends to me)

Through those experiences, I have learned a great deal. I am now in my third marriage of over thirty years, and so I am grateful for what the first two encounters have taught me.

The most important thing I learned related to child raising that is not easy, but so worthwhile, is to never mention the shortcomings of your child's other parent in your child's presence. It does no good to remind them of their shortcomings and you risk them internalizing the sentiment. They will learn for themselves. Just be the best parent you can be. I have always believed that by doing so, you won't project the negative qualities on to the child. I'm not a psychologist; it just makes good sense to me. I would rather them reflect the goodness and kindness of their heavenly Father.

As the stories in this book have shared, God meets our needs, so stand on His promises and principles. Where conventional means will not accommodate and you have given your best, don't act in haste and take things into your own hands; seek God's support and direction. He never fails.

On a September evening almost twenty-five years ago, on a dark street in Pittsburgh's Hazelwood neighborhood, a baby boy was delivered on the front passenger seat of a Geo Metro. This child was not waiting for anything—not his mother to arrive at the hospital or an ambulance to arrive at their location. But although the stage was not set for his delivery in the eyes of any onlooker, God was most definitely in control.

There was a minister and his two teenage sons passing down a cross street, and little did they know what was in store for them. This pregnant woman had run out into the street to find a ride to the hospital when the pastor and his sons spotted her in the street. She ran to them, and when approached, the pastor offered assistance to get her to the hospital but ended up delivering the child instead.

But there was a problem: the umbilical cord was wrapped around the baby's neck. This is where God most definitely intervened, and the pastor with six children himself, although never delivering any one of them and knowing little about childbirth protocols, was able to untwist the cord, and the baby survived. This amazing story was actually published in the Pittsburgh Press about the pastor of the Hilltop Baptist Church (now The Log Church).

But what was not printed in the press was the fact that this child's life was dedicated to Jesus nine months later. Long story short, the mother of this new baby happened to have a drug addiction problem at the time, but through the events of this child's birth and getting introduced to God, she has since come to know and have a personal relationship with Jesus. She knew of God but did not walk with Him in a daily relationship.

After the birth and photographs and news reporters, she was forced to face her plight. From the influences of Pastor Mike and his genuine concern and follow-up, she reached out for help and while in the process, her new child was placed in foster care. She later committed herself to Christ, cleaning up her life, and then moved in a home close to the church. There she also got plenty of support from the entire congregation—financially, emotionally, and spiritually. She then regained custody of her baby boy and remains committed to Christ.

Have you personally had an experience with God that profoundly changed the direction of your life?

If you have, spend time reflecting upon it. You will be blessed every time. Seeing God's hand in the situation is the best inspiration and confirmation of His being with us, walking our walk with us, and overall being engaged in our daily lives.

And it typically takes those situations in our lives to bring us to a point to SEE GOD's influences in our lives. And now, as I recommitted myself to finishing this book solely to support others through their Journey, I experienced a situation in my life that I had never before experienced—I lost my job. A job that I know God blessed me with to care for myself and others—my family, my friends, church, and charities, and to also bring my career to a new level. I truly know this was also His hand in motion. I mentioned this earlier in this chapter, but I want to emphasize its impact on me six years later. To be downsized and have my position eliminated seemed devastating, but through it all, I have this amazing peace.

Some may be bitter by this impact and think this was not of God (How could it be?), but I feel confident that this is God's hand in motion in my life and for my situation, allowing me to have the time and the focus to finish this book before moving to my next new and exciting career adventure. He is so perfectly meeting my needs at this time.

The key is to focus on what is true and wholesome and right. Have you ever heard of the concept of the Power of Intention? It focusses on the concept that both positive and negative forces are out there, and we must choose to focus on the positive and allow God's power to flow though us to impact our own personal Journey in the most positive ways. Making this concept a REALITY as it applies to my relationship with God has been life-changing for me. You just can't imagine the possibilities that lie before us.

To add a bit more rigor on this subject, I was introduced many years ago to a book entitled *The Secret* by Rhonda Byrne. It addresses God as a higher power and recognizes His divine power or energy. I strongly connected with that book, and God has used it in my life to strengthen my relationship with Him as well as to reaffirm to me that I do need to intentionally ask God to meet my needs and provide the desires of my heart in His divine and decisive way.

My interpretation of the essence shared as the Law of Attraction:

- *Accept.* Accept everything you are and nothing you are not. God made you in His own image (ELIMINATE NEGATIVE SELF-PROJECTIONS)
- *Ask.* Ask God for the desires of your heart; after all, He is the author of them when you ask Him to be, right? Be

clear about what you want and need and then emulate it to the best of your ability while you're working in your own strength to get there as well, knowing God is in control.

- *Attract*: Follow the first two concepts and let God do His work on this one. Be open and He will complete it in a positive way.

One testimony of mine in this regard is related to my professional career. I am college-educated, and I have worked hard over many years to do my part to get where I am today professionally. But I still had an underlying sense that my hard work was not fully validated as it related to my respective income. So I asked God for this validation, and at a very specific valuation aligned to my experience and expertise, as well as the current market at that time, God made it happen. This instance amazingly impacted my prayer life—and my life overall. I now address every area of my life with that same intention, knowing and respecting that it is God's provision! **PRAISE REPORT!** I'm not suggesting we pray specifically for money, but moreover, valuation and provision.

With accepting God's gifts, we must also use spiritual discernment. One example of how that might work is that many years ago, when I was single and on my own with my first son, I had a friend whom I met in college—a great lady who was from another country. We became close friends and helped each other out along the way.

And then one day, she asked me if I would marry her brother to get him access to this wonderful country that we live in, the USA. WOW, that was an interesting proposal—being poor and thinking through the offer: If I had done it, I would have been paid a great deal of money and also given a new home. I had to pray hard on that one, and as I did, God made my decision rather clear. He let me know that I should not go through with it. It was not ordained by God and actually would have been illegal. So just be careful, that's all I am saying.

Chapter E = Encourage and Edify...to Build Each Other Up

✦

*Let no corrupt communication proceed out of your
mouth, but that which is good to the use of edifying,
that it may minister grace unto the hearers.*
—Ephesians 4:29

The actual word *encouragement* engulfs my mind, and this book is most certainly being written as a message of encouragement. My attempt in sharing our stories is to help and support each other, edifying those in our sphere of influence. By sharing of ourselves and the experiences in our life's Journey, we ourselves grow to become better equipped to be an encouragement to others.

Through this book's Journey, you have already experienced others who, through their personal walk with Jesus, have come to know that this life's Journey is just as important as the final destination, even more if you realize you have to make a decision in this life to impact the next. I have always been an advocate of recycling, and this concept puts things in an interesting perspective for me. The most awesome all-knowing Lord reaches down at the very level we are on and gently lifts us up in a way in which He knows we can relate (understand)—through encouragement.

The stories I have shared may have come out of another person's lips from their own personal experience, but they are being shared as God's spirit. Through the process of *recycling* our emotion and experience, God can bless others and us in the process. Therefore, when we are struggling through difficult times, we have wisdom as the light to show us the way and comfort us, knowing that God can use our every situation for the good. This is His promise: Romans 8:28 states, "and we know that all things work together for good, for those who are called according to his purpose."

What can be more edifying than a career built on faith? One thing that has been extremely important to me and I believe is my one true calling regardless of where my career has been or takes me in the future is to always demonstrate servant leadership. If you have not heard of this term, it is the fundamental desire to be of service to others. It's a leader who puts away their self-serving inclinations to provide servanthood to the team to ultimately benefit the organization. It's founded on building a sense of community to ultimately achieve successfully meeting organizational goals and objectives.

Some of the attributes of servant leadership include listening, empathy, awareness, foresight, stewardship, and commitment to the growth of people and in building a sense of community. Recorded benefits of this type of leadership style have resulted in stronger teams, a more conducive work environment, improved responsiveness, and motivated employees who truly feel valued—all of which result in a decrease of employee turnover. Employee turnover can be extremely costly to an organization, as I well know, because this is the topic that I wrote about in my thesis in college to obtain my bachelor's degree in human resource management—ironically!

Special thank-you to Mr. Robert K. Greenleaf for popularizing this term and bringing this valuable philosophy to light.

If you think about it, servant leadership is basically Jesus in a nutshell. He was the model of servant leadership. And let's face it, if Jesus Himself was a servant, why would we want to be any different? The Bible stories and words attest, as in Matthew 20:28, "just as the Son of Man did not come to be served, but to serve."

I often wonder what this world would be like if everyone had that same mentality. We would actually get stuff done, get it done more efficiently, and collectively accept it as a gift from the Almighty!

Really finding satisfaction in meeting the needs of others first—try it as a step in OPENNESS and see what you learn.

> Let nothing be done through strife or vain
> glory; but in Lowliness of mind let each esteem
> other better than themselves. (Philippians 2:3)

Even Jesus washed the feet of His disciples as described in John 13:12–15, and though I am grateful for the meaning, and it encourages me, I'm not praying for an opportunity to be washing anyone's feet professionally. LOL.

As a default from my recent role elimination, other than writing this book, I have been searching for a new opportunity; and this time I am going to allow myself to be creative and particular about where I spend my time and energy. I realize at this point in my life that I need to work for an employer or an organization that shares my values. Yes, I also need an opportunity to share the wisdom of my past experience and my skill sets, as well as to allow for me to further my development, but in a culture that is more in line with my faith and beliefs, and to afford me with an opportunity to practice what I preach—faith, hope, and love. As I believe has happened in the past, when I secure my next role, it will also again be God-led, so I am praising him in advance! **PRAISE REPORT!**

But I am human, so after making numerous iterations of my resume and spending countless hours reviewing posted positions and company profiles along with other related diligence in the opportunity hunt, I decided to look at my sister's experience when purchasing a home recently. I can't afford the chase time, so I am handing this over to God and staying focused on writing the book that I definitely know He has called me to complete. And when the door opens for a new opportunity, I will know it is from God and work through the opportunity appropriately at that time. It's a stress-relieving approach!

Jesus tells us in the book of Matthew chapter 6 that we should not worry about anything because as He did for the birds in the sky, He'll provide for us and care for us.

I did, however, make good use of my time to continue to learn and grow and edify myself for my next opportunity. I almost doubled my CEHs (Continued Education Hours) by taking part in several seminars and learning opportunities.

I know that God is most definitely my provider of all things—including encouragement and edification! This is not my religion or religious status; THIS IS MY LIFE. I have a friend in Jesus. I give praise and thanks to those who are confident and strong enough to share their faith in a business setting. After all, God is in control in all areas of our lives, not just the ones we decide He will be. It doesn't make me feel compelled to do business with a particular person or organization if the need isn't there, but it certainly directs me to that person or firm when the need is, as I think there is a higher level of trust out of the gate in regard to an ongoing business relationship. They do what they do for the Lord, not to just please people. AGAIN, SERVANT LEADERSHIP! As John 12:26 says, be a servant of God.

Think about the opportunity to support your colleagues in a genuine, caring way, not with seemingly cutthroat ambitions. I personally tend to trust those with a belief and desire to serve the living God although realistically, I recognize that genuine trust is earned.

On the onset of a recent seminar I attended, I picked up the folder provided that included the class outlines and presenter bios, and what I found made me pleasantly surprised. It was a separate added sheet from the company's founders that stated: "I have concluded the accumulation of wealth is an insufficient reason for living. When I reach the end of my days, I must look backward on something more meaningful than the pursuit of a house, land, machines, and stocks and bonds. Nor is fame of any lasting benefit. I will consider my earthly existence to have been wasted unless I can recall a loving family, a consistent investment in the lives of others, and an earnest to attempt to serve the God who made me—Nothing else makes much sense." (Author Unknown. Shared by Mr. Larry Hendrickson, Founder and Managing Partner at G&H Financial Group) Thank you, Larry, for your courage and love for Jesus in sharing this with the world.

I'm sure you see this type of professed faith all around you, especially when you are looking for it, as there are companies that share their faith vibrantly, like on their building marquees for all to see.

When I lived in the Pittsburgh area, there was a small auto repair shop not far from my home, and I looked forward to driving past their shop just to read the inspirational and uplifting message they displayed in their front window because it made me smile in appreciation of all that God has done for me in my life. And on one occasion when I had car issue, they were the first place I thought to get my repairs. They did live up to their profession and treated me with respect and fairness.

Where I now currently live in Ohio, there is a rather large manufacturing business not far from my home that also shares uplifting messages on their marquee, the most recent one being: "A gentle answer deflects anger, but harsh words make tempers flare." GREAT ADVICE! I would add that even the most honest answers that may not be liked can be delivered gently and with love versus negatively delivered. Let's try to remember to choose our words wisely!

In another interesting interview, I met with a young lady named Danielle. She so elegantly described her relationship with God as "His word is written on my heart." How amazing it has to be to feel that close to your Maker? And yet she feels closest to God when she seriously needs Him. She describes her connection with God as an energy. And because His word is written on her heart, she hears His voice so strongly and so intensely at times. Her belief is that this is how God prepares her for things upcoming, by providing forewarnings or vibes and then direction. It's an amazing gift from God that directs her into the right steps to do the right thing. She totally agrees that it's better to do what is right on the front end even if she is tempted otherwise and spare herself the residual pain later. God's love is imperative to her life.

Danielle is also an avid reader and is typically drawn to inspirational books, books that encourage her connection with God. "It is so important for women to stay connected with each other—to learn and share strength from each other." Her advice is to say thank you for everything, no matter how big or how small, and to always accept a kind word as a gift.

Aligned with the energy theme, I am an avid music listener and appreciator, and in my experience with Christian music, it can definitely be inspiring. But it's not the only inspiring options. I recommend exploring the different types of music out there including mainstream music; just choose what uplifts you and inspires you personally. It's all about balance and what motivates you in a positive way.

Think about what you listen to. How has music affected you?

Below are examples of mainstream music that I have personally made a positive connection:

1. "Lean on Me" by Bill Withers
2. "One Love" by Bob Marley
3. "Three Little Birds" by Bob Marley
4. "Soulshine" by Allman Brothers Band
5. "You Raise Me Up" by Josh Groban
6. "If I Ever Needed Someone" by Van Morrison
7. "Keep Your Head to the Sky" by Earth, Wind & Fire

As I am sharing these, I want to also share one of my all-time favorite Christian songs, which is "Amazing Grace": "Amazing Grace, how sweet the sound, that saved a wretch like me. I once was lost, but now I'm found, was blind but now I see." How beautiful is that?

The following are ways to support your personal inspiration and edification:

- *Daily Bread*: Literally food for your soul! (Our Daily Bread Ministries)
- *Bible study*: A consistent way to get into the Bible and its teachings but also an opportunity to meet with others and fellowship.
- *Prayer groups*: Opportunity to collectively pray for each other and share testimonies—to overall connect spiritually.
- *Daily prayer*: So many people start their day in prayer to get the day off on the right foot mentally (mindset) and then end it to thank God for it!

- *Sunday services*: We attend church on Sunday to learn, grow, and fellowship. There are many types of ministries out there too if you are driven to help others in your community (meals, a ride to the store or food bank or church, running errands, etc.). The key is to follow God's prompting and use the gifts God has blessed you with personally to help others in need or who are hurting.

When I was attending classes at Northside University for nutrition management, I made a connection with one of my colleagues—not just any colleague, but one who was truly genuine and sincere. We helped each other with our workload and became friends. We hit it off initially because we had similar interests. For example, she was a bodybuilder and general health clinician, but the one thing I appreciated the most about her is that she was just always so happy. She later introduced me to the reason why she was always so HAPPY.

It started when she introduced me the church she was attending. It was in a neighborhood on the other side of town, but it was most definitely well worth the commute. This was a Bible-believing Christian church, and I embraced the message, as it was what I had learned as a kid when I accepted Jesus into my life. I was, however, careful and cautious since I had a life-changing experience at the last church I attended. But I did seem to know immediately that this church was different. It was a loving community that wanted nothing but to be there to support others as an extension of Christ. (Interestingly enough, I still belong to that church today, and I am blessed that they have online services because that definitely supports my CEHs (Continuing *Edification* Hours) from one hundred miles away). Thank you, Colleen, for being open to sharing God's love and changing lives. You certainly played a part in saving mine! **PRAISE REPORT!**

There are so many influencers in our lives who support what direction we take, either positive or negative to our outcomes. One woman shared with me an intimate experience about her abortion decision as a teenager. This woman felt guilt in her heart for many years for ending this innocent life, and even more after she actually had a son of her own. But she has prayed for forgiveness and then, realizing God's love, has taken that guilt and turned it into a passion. She now uses that experience as a ministry to share her emotional battle with other young women who can't forgive themselves or are contemplating abortion so they can be prepared for the potential emotional side effects. **PRAISE REPORT!**

I have utmost respect for those who can take these types of experiences and make them into a true blessing and encouragement, to literally use their pain to help and support other, and potentially help them to avoid the pain and negative consequential trade-off in their future.

We walk among so many who make life better. One well-known encouragement spreaders whom I have leaned on in my life is Norman Vincent Peale, as it's no secret that he was quite the motivator and positive thinker. He is the author of *The Power of Positive Thinking* and was a motivational speaker, but I was amazed at how often he relates back to the Bible and its teachings in his works; but I was not surprised at all since he was a reformed minister. The Bible shares the importance of having visions and affirmations; there are multitudes of them addressed. God has definitely used this forum to provide direction in my daily walk. These daily quick reads have been my foundational point of inspiration.

I met a woman named Eve who claimed to be of Christian faith for over twenty-three years. She admitted having a roller-coaster relationship with God, again, like many others interviewed for this book. Generally, her life was easy until the first year into her marriage. Although the details were still too raw to share at that time, she experienced her first real relationship crisis. This crisis caused her to feel more distant from God, as well as experience low self-esteem and worthlessness—what most would describe as depression. She became so ill that she was throwing up, having panic attacks, and even putting herself into a fetal position and could not leave the house. As this experience happened, deep in her heart, she knew that she had to reengage more closely with God while working out her relationship with her husband. Reading Bible scriptures and communing with God in daily prayer greatly helped, and she became even closer to God, which ultimately influenced her self-esteem being brought more of a healthy humbleness. She now knows and considers this her salvation experience because this is when she knowingly asked Jesus into her heart and life. **PRAISE REPORT!** God uses our pain to generate blessings!

Eve's Thailand experience happened shortly after this crisis and turned around her life and seriously solidified her relationship with Christ. She feels this is what brought her closest to God—ministering to orphaned and disabled children. What she learned is that success is from just being there, not necessarily "saving the day". She used to think that being a Christian was an easy road, because, after all, GOD is always just there, right? But it's really not; it's a Journey with its own ups and downs, happiness and sadness, successes and failures, and that's how we grow! Through her experiences with anxiety and depression, she is now able to help others with these same issues. **PRAISE REPORT!**

Many years back, I was scheduled to speak at a local women's ministry when writing this book. I had hoped to have finished most of it by that time, but I had not. Unknowingly to me at that time, God had more experiences and stories for me to share. As it goes, I was tempted to cancel my testimony due to surrounding pressures, but I knew this book was Jesus-led. So I just stepped out in faith and did not cancel. The spirt led me to that point, and I had to trust regardless of the outcome. Even though *my* plans for completion of the book were not on track, ultimately, God's was and that had to be my focus. To mark the occasion, I created homemade bookmarkers that shared the Bible verse that this book is based on, Romans 8:28, and give them a takeaway to remind them of the message. This is a picture of the "homemade" bookmark that I shared in 1997.

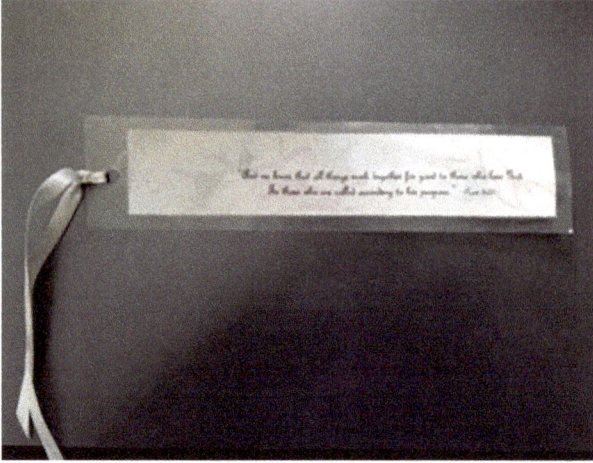

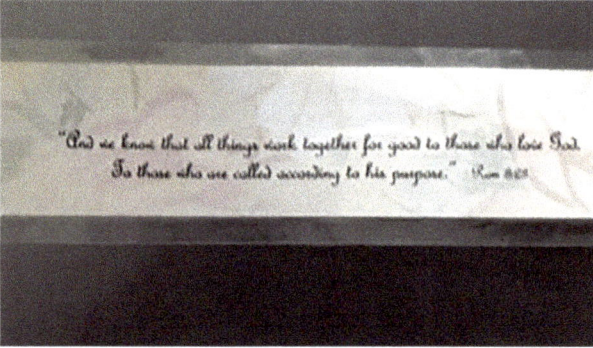

"And we know that all things work together for good to those who love God. To those who are called according to his purpose." Rom 8:28

I have learned throughout my life that doing God's will is far more exciting, interesting, and valuable than not taking that step in faith and experiencing His "bringing it back to my attention." And now with a more experienced perspective, I don't want to experience that too often, so I act on His prompting as much as possible to bless others and know that I am in the will of God. The Holy Spirit of God is a vital part of this relationship. God promises that when you receive His free gift of salvation, you receive FULL ACCESS to His Holy Spirit. Choose to be Spirit-led and Spirit-filled daily! First, know that salvation is a PRICELESS gift from God; it can't be bought or earned. It must be received in your heart.

Whose life have you touched today? Call a friend, pray together, share a meal!

Another great story I just have to share is about LaShawn, an amazing friend who was once in my life, and I know now she was put there by God. We were introduced by our mothers who had worked together at some point. When we first met, she was in high school, and I was in need of a babysitter for my oldest son. She turned out to be an awesome babysitter and friend. In fact, she was around so much that we all eventually started calling her Nanny. She is younger than me, but so much wiser. She taught me that God's plan is sufficient. During our interview, she shared that sometimes things work out great, and she is grateful, and sometimes not so great, but she knows in her heart because of her relationship with Jesus that there has to be a reason, especially when you make decisions for things in your control the best that you can with the information you have. (Her comments reminded me of what my mother shared with me as well.) God knows, and that's what is most important.

She stated that her life was a testament and witness of the power of prayer. LaShawn kept a prayer journal and frequently updated it. She used this to read the miracles and answered prayers from her past to refresh her sense of God's presence in her life. "God has given us feelings and emotions, and we exercise those for various reasons, but they are not to be discouraging. For example, like crying, hurting, or being upset—these are also gifts because they help us to redirect or just get cleansed internally and ready to start a new."

Later in life LaShawn married a great guy, and the witness of her faith was used by God in helping him to also understand God's power. It took a few years, but little by little, he began to trust in God. In my opinion, since men typically seem to want to be the "fixer," it must be tougher for them to relinquish all to God's will—just sayin'.

She shared a story with me about her past that involved her abusive and judgmental mother. This was a big reason she grew up insecure and had a low self-esteem, and there was a lot of pain tied to these memories. She always felt like she was living in the shadow of her mother's opinions. Her mother was a professing Christian, but unfortunately, she wasn't living in God's power to have allowed this mental abuse to occur. The detail in this story is that LaShawn is biracial, and her white mother had a bad experience with her black father. And since she lived with her mother and rarely had an opportunity to see her father, in her mind, she felt as though she was being punished for that relationship…even by her own skin color. It was a constant reminder to her mother of her past. Her mother was by this time remarried to a white man, and they attended a Christian church regularly.

Let me take a moment here and make a statement. Just because someone goes to church does not mean they are living in God's will. If you get one thing out of this book, let it be this—God loves us all, and we should be honored to carry that same sentiment by truly loving others. God's love can be manifested in many ways, but kindness is always a start.

Getting back to LaShawn's story, one day, after a major family feud, LaShawn cried out to God to be released from what she considered the imprisonment that she felt was holding her in bondage—her color. She immediately felt His peace and knew that God's view of her was all that was important. She began to love herself as God loved her, which was an incredible blessing because in my eyes, LaShawn was the most beautiful—in mind, heart, and spirit! **PRAISE REPORT!**

Her path is in praying daily, and she would share that it's not only when you wake up, or not just when you see an insect on your counter, or when you are so broke that you can only afford a trailer to reside. GIVE THANKS for what you DO have.

LaShawn prays continually throughout the day for the desires of her heart and admits that as she seeks God's will in her life. Sometimes those desires may change, but it's all part of the process of leaning on and trusting God for her best interest.

LaShawn's mantra is that "Each day is different, nothing is more satisfying than being in God's will, and there's always a beyond yourself. New beginning, new day—God gives you what you need." Let's face it, life can be gone in an instant; but it doesn't matter because there is an afterlife with God. She truly lives for more than what this world has to offer.

As a youth who had everything material but lacked emotional support, these material things made no difference. A bit later in her life, when we had this interview, she was living in subsidy housing, and you would think she was at the lowest point of her life; but she was in a great place with God, knowing she was rich beyond belief. Today, LaShawn has come a long way. She has a college degree and is a well-respected contributor to her family and her community.

As a true confession, the one major regret that I have is not attending her father's funeral. See, I had gotten to know her father during our friendship, and he was a great, fun person and treated me wonderfully. But his funeral was at a time that I was struggling with my brain tumor diagnosis and could not bring myself to her aid in a time of her grief; it felt too close to me. It's a decision I have long regretted, as I believe it led to a distance between our relationship over the years. I miss her much and sadly missed the opportunity to see her beautiful family grow up. A true regret on my part, but I know she is in God's hands and making a difference in this world!

LEARN: Get outside of yourself and your own issues. We will, on occasion, have to do uncomfortable things in this life to support others. Know that God is by your side to give you the strength to do the right thing.

There is an inspiring quote that I was exposed to long ago when I was in a situation in my career that I thought was a good move. Having a degree in human resources, I moved to the HR Department to fulfill what I thought was the career I should be in. And although I had colleagues who were supportive, the situation became painful. I was working for a manager who reported to our VP and they were both negative people. They were not encouraging at all, and in fact, they put me down every chance they could get, thinking that might motivate me—NOT.

Fortunately, the Lord brought a message to me that prompted me to take action, and I decided to move back into procurement and have since learned over the past twenty years that it is where my career truly needed to be. When I was in this role, another colleague shared an interesting Mark Twain quote with me that influenced my own leadership values. The verse goes like this: "Keep away from people who try to belittle your ambitions. Small people always do that. But the really great ones make you feel that you too can become great." (Thank you, Elaine!) God used this experience to help me to continue to grow and has connected me with a lot of great people and influencers in my life as well. With that, He has allowed me to be a positive influence in others' lives—so important.

This topic reminds me of a sermon I had once heard my church pastor share in the late nineties (Thanks, Pastor Mike!). It's around four influencing areas of life that we are all susceptible to, which can cause discouragement. And if we can avoid these four areas, we have a better chance to experience and share encouragement with others. I've added my input as "Antidotes" aligned to each area:

1. *Fatigue*: Physical tiredness can definitely increase your chances of experiencing worry and stress, both physically and mentally.

   Antidote: Work hard and stay focused on the positive and always lift up your fears and concerns to God daily. Lift them up knowing that God is listening.

   Work hard, worry less—FAITH OVER FEAR!

   SUPPORTING IDEA: I created a Prayers and Praises box this year, and it has amazingly strengthened my prayer life. I took a rather large shoebox, covered it in uplifting wrapping paper, cut a slit in the top, and set it on my kitchen counter. I see it first thing in the morning when getting my coffee, and I keep a pen and paper in a small basket next to it so I have everything set up to lift my prayers and praises to God, not just in the morning but throughout the day when the Spirit moves me, or a call or text for prayer arrives, if I wake up from a sleep with someone strongly on my mind, and so forth. I write my prayers and praises on the paper—there's something about writing them—and then put them in the box, knowing God is hearing them.

2. *Frustration*: This can creep in at any time, especially in situations where you feel things are out of your control. We all have a past and carry that baggage with us because these are experiences that form a lot of our thoughts even years later.

Antidote: Dump the garbage truck and start each day fresh and new. Your past decisions and actions were hopefully all made with the information you had at the time you had to make them.

PERSONAL REFLECTION: When I was pregnant with my third son, I was frustrated because I was already a struggling single mom taking care of my first two sons. I wasn't sure how I would make this work even though I was blessed to have the long-distance support of his father. And although quite embarrassed, I called my mother to share the news. At the start of the conversation, she could feel my frustration, but she listened and then provided caring words that I still remember to this day. She said that she thanked God we were talking life, and that was a beautiful thing. She also gave me wisdom that I lean back on pretty regularly and that is that "we can only make our decisions with the information we have at the time, and that's the best anyone can ask for." Let's face it, there is only so much we can truly control.

3. *Failure*: Not reaching our goals is no reason to stop striving for the better. If you listen to testimonies from a lot of great athletes, you will learn that failure is a precursor to success. You have to keep trying, and sometimes that requires working and praying harder.

    Antidote: Spend time in prayer regularly and really connect with God. He is your Creator and knows you the best. My prayers are my way of speaking to God throughout the day, along with my writings that I put into my Prayers and Praises box. I have to reiterate that there is something special about actually writing these shares to God. But when I am driving, working, playing, visiting, and so forth, my thoughts and spoken words are lifted to God, and I know He hears them as well.

4. *Fear*: God promises a safe landing but not always smooth sailing, and it's normal to experience fear. This is when we need to stand on God's promises to trust and obey. Fear

is actually a gift because it is our body's way of telling us that something is wrong and we need to do something to protect it.

Antidote: Trust in God to take these fears and use them for your good. In some way, there needs to be some protection or action. Let the action begin with seeking God's counsel.

A huge fearful experience in my life happened many years back. I was experiencing abnormal sensations across my face and numbness in my leg causing minor tripping incidents. Realizing this was not normal, I went to my primary care physician with these concerns. At this point, I wasn't sure what could be causing these symptoms, but I knew it wasn't normal. After a consultation and some testing, I received a call on April 1 of that year from my doctor. She called me because she was heading out for vacation that same day and had just received my test results and wanted me to take some next steps that she didn't want delayed. She then began to explain to me that I had a petroclival meningioma in my brain. I was at work at the time and immediately typed that description into my computer as she was speaking…and in large font, all I could see was BRAIN TUMOR. Talk about fear, that will do it!

She explained that this tumor was on my brain stem and was the reason I was experiencing these symptoms. I took a deep breath and then took her advice to consult with a neurologist. She gave me the referrals and asked me to work with her staff to set up the appointment.

This experience in and of itself was quite a Journey. Thank God I was already grounded in my relationship with Christ, or I am not sure how I would have responded to this news. Yes, I experienced fear—fear of my life ending much sooner that I would have liked. I wanted to experience my kids growing up and graduating from high school and then college, getting married, having my sweet, beautiful grandkids. My hopeful world flashed in front of me, and I decided to reprioritize.

After seeking several opinions on treatment, I learned a great deal—nonoperative or high-risk surgery that could result in death, paralysis, blindness, and the like—interesting options, but after much prayer and research, I decided to wait until my symptoms were worse than my risks. Special thanks to a neurosurgeon I sought for one of my second opinions who was out of the Cleveland Clinic. He spoke to me in a straightforward and businesslike yet compassionate way! I then booked a family trip to Disney World and the next year to Hawaii—I was actualizing my own personal bucket list.

Long story short, after a few years of monitoring the growth of the tumor, I decided to work with an oncology radiation doctor and his team at AGH in an attempt to stop the growth that was beginning to get large enough to impede my neurological system. It required two months of daily radiation treatments. This was the mask I was snapped into on the radiation table for each of those appointments. I kept it to keep perspective!

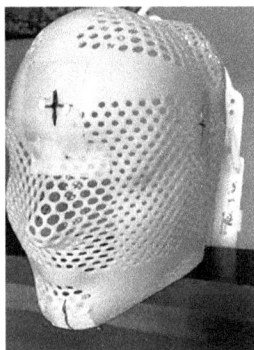

I was grounded in my relationship with God at this time and used each session to pray for others as I was flaunted by the prayer shawl my aunt Dale knitted for me when she heard of my decision (Thank you, Aunt Dale!). The compassionate radiation nurses draped it over me after getting me situated in the radiation machine.

After this treatment, I was praising the Lord even more gratefully, as I learned that the brain tumor had stopped growing. And not only that, it had actually shrunk by 20 percent, which we were not expecting to happen, but it did. **PRAISE REPORT!** Every step of this multiyear experience was fearful, yet I felt peace, and I know that this peace was from God. The relationship I had established over the years had made this a true blessing.

And I never stopped working throughout my treatments. I would get my radiation in the early morning, and then make it to work by 9:00 a.m. FOCUS (and a few distractions) is everything! And when I finished this round of radiation therapy, my supportive and generous leadership team at Heinz wanted to do something special for me to support my survival (Thank you, Dewann!). I could have bought myself something new, went on a vacation, or whatever, but after thinking through and praying about their generous offer, I decided that the best way to honor my survival was to somehow show gratitude to the hospital team that helped me in my time of need. To show appreciation for all they had done for me, I arranged for a special lunch brought to them right there in their office. I chose this because I prayed about it, and that was where God led me.

The good news is I am still here today, ten years later, writing this book that God led for me to write to inspire and edify YOU! **PRAISE REPORT!** And I have no related debt, as my medical insurance covered 100 percent of the related treatment cost. **PRAISE REPORT!**

To add some interesting background to this story, several months into interviewing many women for this book, I began to experience what I referred to as brain surges—something I had never experienced in the past (or in the future for that matter). They were hard to describe, like electrical impulses intermittently surging through my brain.

After three weeks of experiencing these surges and multiple doctor appointments, I found myself being admitted to the hospital, as my doctor detected what she thought was an infection based on medical testing results that were performed tied to my described symptoms: EEG and CAT Scan.

It was later that afternoon, after spending all morning getting this testing completed, when I finally made it back home. Upon arrival home, I clicked on the answering machine to hear my messages (yes, that was the way we did it back then) and began to pour myself some juice as I listened to familiar voices—and then two messages at the end saying, "Hi, Wendy, this is your doctor. I received your test results, and it is important that you call me back immediately." She provided me with the phone numbers to call back and urged me again to call back immediately.

I immediately called back and was quickly redirected to my doctor. As I waited momentarily, I could feel my heart beating strongly; my adrenaline was definitely flowing, as I just knew something was wrong based on their tone of voice. When she picked back up, she told me there were abnormal results that needed to be addressed right away and I was to come back down to the hospital. I was told "Don't make calls, don't eat anything, just get back here so we can see you again." *Oh well, I guess I am sick*, I thought although the day prior, the brain surge symptoms had seemed to stop, and I thought I was actually getting better.

I immediately called my husband and then my mother and quickly told them what was up and asked them to meet me at the hospital. I was so consumed with thinking about what might be wrong that I couldn't think about anything else—including my drive back to the hospital. I made it safely despite my apprehension.

Ron made it there simultaneously upon my arrival as I was whisked away to a triage room. Then my mother soon after showed up, and I explained to her the little I knew to that point. Then my doctor entered the room. She sat down and began explaining the test results to us. "You have a very serious brain infection called encephalitis, and the only way to treat this viral infection is with IV antiviral medication, which means you will need to stay in the hospital for a couple weeks to be treated and watched." It appears a twenty-one-day IV med treatment was required. "This is a very serious condition and can be fatal," she stated. Then she continued to explain that there would be a lot of doctors following my case to support. With that, as you could imagine, my husband and mother had fear written all over their faces. But strangely enough, I literally felt a relief and a presence of peace come over me, as after weeks of this experience, I finally received a diagnosis, and something was being done to help me.

Things were happening too fast, and at this point, my doctor introduced me to two other doctors who were taking over my care. And then the IV team came into the room to get my IV started. My patient room was now ready, and as we were awaiting the wheelchair to take me there, room 1197-2, I found myself comforting my mother and my husband. I could honestly feel God's peace and wanted them too as well. I looked at this hospital stay as some free time to work on writing the book.

As things settled, my mother left to help us by picking up and taking care of the kids, and Ron went home to get my necessities for the hospital stay. I remember teasing the attendant who was pushing my noisy wheelchair up to my room. I referred to him as my chauffeur, and we chatted lightly the rest of the way to the eleventh floor.

When we arrived, I met my nurse and then got settled in my room. Soon after, many other doctors with different specialties came in to ask me questions—neurology, general medicine, infectious disease, you name it! I was feeling quite popular. Then Dr. Indide showed up (turns out this name actually means "patience"). She was a young doctor with a bright smile. How would you not remember that?

Soon after, I was taken to get a spinal tap, but after several attempts and getting no fluid, they had to take me the X-ray department to perform this invasive test, as this would give them the visibility to perform more accurately. This process was NOT FUN and actually intensely painful, but the X-ray sure did help. I remember getting charley horses as the fluid drained into their syringe...and then the immediate headache. I was advised to sleep on my back or side for the rest of the night to help alleviate the side effects of head pressure and associated pain.

When I had returned to my room, I was told that I just missed Pastor Mike's visit but that he would try to return later. Now that this further testing had been completed and I was tired, Ron left to get the kids and relieve my mother. I remember being so hungry at this point, as I realized I hadn't eaten the entire day. Around nine in the evening, they took me down to get an MRI. It was so crazy how many people I actually knew at that local neighborhood hospital, but it was comforting as they tried to make light of the situation on my behalf.

As I lay in the hallway on a stretcher, awaiting my turn, I observed an elderly woman doing the same…although she was moaning a great deal. And then as I watched the techs move her to another stretcher, I was cracking up as she had been moved so quickly that it appeared she had flown on to the new stretcher. But then her moaning became bone-chilling. I then thought to myself not to laugh because that was cruel, and yet it was hysterical to watch.

And then I started to think about my turn and what they would do with me. I have to admit I was happy to see her stretcher move out of that area, as the sounds were loud and distressing. When my turn arrived, it was a different situation. I sat right up and walked to the MRI machine happily. I so did not want to live out that same performance with me playing the lead role (LOL).

The tech was gracious, and the testing did not take that long, and before I knew it, I was back in my room. It was late, and I was tired; and as I was just settling in, Dr. Indide returned. It turned out that she had gone home but could not get my case out of her mind, so she returned to do my case history. We spent a good hour and a half talking, and amazingly, I was able to share my Christian testimony with her. Afterward, she found me some graham crackers before she left. I was so hungry, and so thankful. **PRAISE REPORT!**

During this entire situation, I tried to talk positively to every-one I came in contact with because I didn't want to be a gray cloud.

At six in the morning the next day, I was awakened by a needle. "Are you sure I need this?" I questioned the technician. "What is it? Who ordered it? Does my doctor know you are giving this to me?" If you know me, you know I ask a lot of questions *all the time*. And to my defense, that's just how I learn, but in this case, it was to verify if I needed the shot. After that incident, I was already awake, so I got up and cleaned myself up, put on a little makeup and cleaned my room. Can you tell I was still feeling rather normal?

Shortly after getting back into bed to rest, my curtain was abruptly pulled back, and a voice said, "Are you the Wendy Gill I grew up with?" Lo and behold… I couldn't believe my eyes. It was

Regina, my very first childhood friend. Could this be true? Pinch me. We were reunited after twenty-plus years. She looked so great and treated me amazingly. We spent as much time as possible over the next two days getting reacquainted, although she was on duty, so our time was limited and not nearly enough. We exchanged phone numbers, and it turned out she lived in my extended neighborhood. We were only four parallel streets away from each other. How weird was that? And we never ran into each other at a grocery store, the library, a park, wherever—so strange that it took this situation to be reconnected. From that moment, I realized why my visit to AGH happened. If only to be reunited, it was worth it all. **PRAISE REPORT!**

That day seemed to be extremely long as I awaited test results, received many calls from friends, a few visitors, and multiple doctor visits sprung on me. But I was elated about seeing Regina, and I shared it with everyone thereafter, and later learned so did she.

Later that evening, I was told that my preliminary spinal tap results were normal, except for some undetermined cultures, and the brain MRI showed no abnormalities. All I could think of was YES, no brain damage! **PRAISE REPORT!**

Then the neurology team arrived, asking me over and over about the brain surges I experienced. This team was led by a very notable doctor, as he was the best in the Burgh I understood, as my sister-in-law who was well connected in the medical world recommended him. Interestingly enough, based on my medical history, labs, and diagnostic testing results, he wasn't convinced as how to diagnose me and felt that I may have been initially misdiagnosed. Remember, at this point, I was not getting the surges any longer, as they subsided a day prior to my admittance. His "wild guess"—stress-induced seizures.

At this point, they began to stop my medicine at my request, as it was not jiving right with my system. They tried another medication, and that was worse; it spaced me out. Throughout that evening, I had multiple visitors, people who genuinely cared about me, including my kids, and thank God because I missed them so much at this point.

After they left, I was tired and finally fell asleep. Then about two hours later, at approximately eleven thirty that evening, the room lights go on. And then I heard this terrible moaning sound. WAIT… I knew that sound, as it was so familiar. NO, it couldn't be. But it was, the moaner from MRI, and she kept me up until at least two in the morning. You just got to love God's sense of humor, and this was one of those demonstrations of it. Be careful what you laugh about.

I was tired of all the attention, well, medical attention, and no real confirmed or treatable problem at this point, so I asked my doctor to please release me and let me go home. She eventually agreed but needed Neurology to approve. When Neurology arrived, they tried another medication, but it made me sicker, and then they agreed to release me medication-free! They trusted my response that I would come back in a heartbeat if the surges or any other symptom returned. But as we talked before my actual release, ironically enough, they randomly asked me what my religion was. THIS OPENED A BIG DOOR, and I was able to explain my faith and the endeavor I had accepted from God to write an inspirational book. **PRAISE REPORT!** And I promised her a copy and will keep that promise when published.

As you can imagine, by this time I was so sick and tired of explaining my previous symptoms. I just couldn't wait to get back to my home sweet home. By five that afternoon, I was released and back at home. Yes, I surprised them all, thanks to God and His healing power. My church family was so generous and brought meals to my home for days after I returned. What an amazing gift. I also received calls, cards, flowers, and the like. Talk about feeling special! THANK you to all my friends at that time. You truly made me feel special and blessed! For a change, I had to sit back and allow others to do for me, so I learned from this experience to do it gratefully.

Although I actually had peace during this situation, I began to look at life even more differently. It's what happens to you when you are faced with a possible deadly diagnosis situation, later to learn that there were many others praying for me. My mother had added me to every prayer list possible—her church, my church, all her Christian friends, her weekly prayer group, and so forth. God literally carried me through that experience physically, mentally, emotionally, and spiritually. And as you read, He provided me with amazing gifts along the way.

I remember speaking with a friend Lex when I got home, and I shared with her that I literally touched the robe of Jesus, as I truly believe I was healed. Another story of God's ever-present peace—and yes, I do believe that God is the Great Physician, and He does work through our hardworking medical teams when needed, but I'm convinced this one was His touch! **PRAISE REPORT!**

At this point, I didn't care to ask God why. I have been there too many times. I didn't ask for anything. I just knew in my heart His will was being accomplished, and I anticipated the why being revealed in His time, if He so desired. It was just a privilege and an honor to be used by Him, and that is true excitement to my soul. I was at such peace that I literally thanked Him through the entire experience, even for the moaner despite the irony! It was by God's divine intervention that I was so positive through that situation. He will never leave you nor forsake you—that was my hands-on experience. I can't share that to the medical world, as they typically deal with the facts and test results. But with that, it all proves no other explanation possible. They couldn't find one, so they adlibbed a diagnosis.

As a close to this story, I ended up leaving the beautiful purple flowers that were bought for me while in the hospital to my roommate (Helen), and to her it was a huge blessing, and then unknowingly to come home and have the same beautiful flowers delivered to me from a friend. (Thank you, Lex) **PRAISE REPORT!**

The point here is that with all the ways that discouragement can creep up on us, weeding its way into our lives and potentially tripping us up from God's will and plan for us, we need to hold closer to God, spending time to nurture the relationship with prayer and connection. These opportunities should be seen as important reasons to pull us closer to God instead of becoming overwhelmed and pulling away. I know and have experienced it in my life that God can use these seemingly negative events to do great, positive things. Just don't give up and look for Him in everything.

Edification tip: Something more to ponder: If you let something, some thought or desire, consume you, it's not from God. Alternatively, let God consume you and His will is perfected through you!

Try staying organized, I have learned that it helps keep my mind clear. Meet with God regularly in daily conversation, resist a bad attitude regardless of the reason or reasons (I have to remind myself of this one a lot), put on a positive attitude daily—just like putting on your clothes in the morning—and stay focused on the future and the amazing things God is going to help you with throughout your day and, ultimately, your life.

Now, with all the craziness that this world has been through over the last couple years with COVID-19, it's been even more important for me personally to stay connected with God on a daily basis. There just seems to be a lot more negativity out there, which I am associating with people's fears.

One thing that I began doing to physically remove bad or negative thoughts from my mind as they try to creep in is this physical antidote (you may want to adopt one in your own special way too). When I am getting thoughts that are not uplifting or worrisome, I start this action to shake my head to the left three times. I'm not sure how this initially came about, but it is definitely working for me. It is an action between myself and God, and by doing that physical motion, I am giving this concern or worry over to God because I know I cannot carry it.

I shared these three shakes to the left with a colleague of mine and their response was incredible. They shared with me that they also started a similar action because they too needed to let go of worry in this time of uncertainty. One friend in particular mentioned that his was a different type of head movement, which I found interesting, similar to mine but still unique to him. He shared this with his spouse and was told that a psychologist once told her that doing something physical is the best way to offset negative thoughts (I actually had no idea but was glad for the validation). Try your own style of giving this over to God in a physical way that keeps you connected to Him throughout the day.

What it truly comes down to is that we need to listen to God's voice. So pray for God's voice, ask Him to speak to you directly. There are so many competing voices out there. Listen to God's voice and He will take you where you need to be, places you can't yet fathom, places we can't see through the storms and the clouds…where you will be truly the happiest.

One tool I have found inspiring and thought-provoking for my own walk with God is a spiritual booklet called *Our Daily Bread*. This pocket-size reading has been wonderfully refreshing for me. It's a great way to start the day, or end the day, or anytime in between. If you are not familiar with it, it is made up of one pager Bible reflections for each day of the month, and each booklet contains three months of thought-provoking edification. Even better, they are free for the asking. Just reach out to Our Daily Bread Ministries to make a request.

Chapter Y = Your Yield and the Fruits of the Spirit

✦

When you yield to the living God, you are surrendering your more worldly desires and choosing to have God's will perfected through you so that you can produce a steadfast harvest, continue to bear fruit, to share blessings, and to be blessed. It's like choosing to become a new creature daily through God's grace and forgiveness (2 Corinthians 5:17). As you start each new day, take a minute to commune with God by thinking positive and asking the Lord to soften your heart so He can plant fruitful seeds.

On the subject of yielding to God to ultimately yield fruit in your life, my sister more recently experienced an interesting situation, which resulted into an amazing testimony that needs to be shared. She was house-hunting fervently because she was in a shared rental situation, but now it was time to get on her own two feet and into her own space. She had looked for several months, as she had been savings for years for the day—the day she would be an independent homeowner.

As she began her search, the property market began to increase quite quickly. She was working with a real estate agent, although anything she had looked at in her price range needed further investment and a lot of work to make livable, or it was just not the right fit. Along with the market acceleration, the interest rates were also climbing, which was a huge consideration financially.

Finally, after spending a lot of time searching high and low, she realized that it just wasn't the right time and decided to end her search although her search had been prayerfully lifted. She called her realtor back after doing her last walk through that morning and advised her that she was no longer looking, and they ended their house-hunting relationship.

Now that she had stopped looking, assuming it was just not the right time, this is when God had the opportunity to work and to let her know He was in control. The next day, she received a phone call from a friend who knew she had been searching for the right home. She mentioned that a condo unit in her area of interest was going to be on the market soon, and she wondered if she might be open to checking it out. Prayerfully, my sister agreed, and that same evening, she arrived at the unit for a walk-through with the owner. Quickly into the walkthrough, she just knew it was the "one." It was in the right location, had a parking garage, extra storage, just needed a small amount of work to move in (cleaning and painting basically), and as a side bonus, a maintained swimming pool. But most importantly, it was in a safe community. WOW, it was everything she had been asking God for in her prayers.

This all led to a conversation with the owners of the estate, and they were open to her making an offer before they placed it on the ever-rising market. After further reviewing her financial situation, determining what she could afford including HOA fees, taxes, and current interest rates, she made a fair offer that she knew she could afford.

After making the offer, she remained hopeful, but as negativity always tries to creep in, she thought maybe they would come back with a counteroffer that she could not swing. But she was wrong, and God was truly working on her behalf. They did come back with a counteroffer, but it was minimal and actually was her budgetary limit. She ended up buying the home under market value and not having to pay added realtor fees. This all played a part in making this perfect home affordable—far beyond her initial expectation. She will tell you to this day that God gets all the credit. She attributes this situation working out to her finally letting go and giving God control. **PRAISE REPORT!**

After sharing this story with her contact who initially introduced her to this new home, the woman heartfully stated that she was humbled to be used as an instrument in executing God's plan. Throughout the entire encounter, my sister claimed a promise she had from God in her heart: "You saw me to it; you'll see me through it." **PRAISE REPORT!**

This is a perfect example of doing what it takes but allowing God to take control. We still need to do our part, but by just being open to the possibilities and God's leading, doors open. In her situation, she had to stop her fruitless searching and let God work, a true testament that we need to truly trust in God for ALL areas of our lives.

When you yield to God's leading for your life, He blesses you with fruits of the Spirit. In 1 Corinthians 12:7, God shares that "the manifestation of the Spirit is given to every man to profit withal." And then again in 1 Corinthians 14, God actually tells us to desire these spiritual gifts. I internalize the following list of gifts, as shared in the Word of God, as tools from God to help us along in our Journey and to help others along in theirs.

1. *Love*—1 Corinthians 13:4–8: "Love is patient and kind; love does not envy or boast; it is not arrogant or rude. It does not insist on its own way; it is not irritable or resentful; it does not rejoice at wrongdoing, but rejoices with the truth. Love bears all things, believes all things, hopes all things, endures all things. Love never ends." REFLECTION: Christine and Chad's story—Valentine's Day Gift of Salvation

2. *Joy*—Proverbs 15:23: "A man hath joy by the answer of his mouth: and a word spoken in due season, how good is it!" REFLECTION: Vicki's new home story—To God be the Glory

3. *Peace*—John 16:33: "I have told you these things, so that in me you may have peace. In this world you will have trouble. But take heart! I have overcome the world." Have you heard the saying, "To know Jesus is to Know Peace"

(or) more abruptly, "No Jesus, No Peace"? REFLECTION: The peace that was felt when I was in the hospital, being told I had a life-threatening infection, and God gave me this peace to be a strong witness.

4. *Patience*—Romans 12:12: "Be joyful in hope, patient in affliction, faithful in prayer." Learn to exercise patience as a conscious decision, as I have learned, when I pray for patience, I experience opportunities to exercise it. REFLECTION: Think of Melony's beautiful story and the patience it took to restore her marriage.

5. *Kindness*—Ephesians 4:32 KJV: "And be ye kind one to another, tenderhearted, forgiving one another, even as God for Christ's sake hath forgiven you." REFLECTION: It takes kindness to think of others in a time of need. Let the stories of meeting others' needs be examples of how when you help another, you are already blessed!

6. *Goodness*—Galatians 6:10: "Therefore, as we have opportunity, let us do good to all people, especially to those who belong to the family of believers." REFLECTION: If you recall the story of Eve and the goodness she performs, helping children by God's leading as a direct result of her painful experiences.

7. *Faithfulness*—Proverbs 28:20: "A faithful person will be richly blessed, but one eager to get rich will not go unpunished." Christians with this spiritual gift trust in God's sovereignty and put their life in His hands. REFLECTION: All the women who shared their stories are demonstrating their faithfulness to God in one way or another, tied to their individuality and uniqueness.

8. *Gentleness* (Not to be confused with weakness)—1 Peter 3:15: "But in your hearts sanctify Christ as Lord. Always be prepared to give a defense to everyone who asks you the reason for the hope that is in you. But respond with gentleness and respect." REFLECTION: Think about the message that was posted by a local business to share their faith

with God: "A Gentle Answer Deflects Anger, but Harsh Words Make Tempers Fly."

9. *Self-control*—Romans 12:2: "Do not conform to the pattern of this world, but be transformed by the renewing of your mind. Then you will be able to test and approve what God's will is—his good, pleasing and perfect will." REFLECTION: In my interview with Amy, she shared a compelling comment about her children and her responsibility to them: "You're either brainwashing them with the world and its influences without your control, or you are brainwashing them with more wholesome things and to know and aspire to have a relationship with Jesus."

As each has received a gift, use it to serve one another, as good stewards of God's varied grace. (1 Peter 4:10 ESV)

What fruit is your life producing, healing and healthy or harmful and negative?

Your personal faith is a testimony, and as you face life difficulties with contentment and a gentle spirit, you are a witness to all who know you.

DREAM BIG—you serve a BIG GOD. Do you know your calling from God? It's not a one and done, my friend. If an undertaking does not include faith, perhaps it's not worthy of being called God's direction. There's this old saying, "Even a turtle doesn't get ahead unless he sticks his neck out." Small matters have their place, but spend the majority of your time on the steps of faithfulness. Choose today to dream big and strive to reach the full potential of your calling.

Knowing Jesus as your personal Savior is the first step in the Journey. Ask him in your heart today and claim His promises. Start realizing His power in your life. It's a gift and is here for the taking.

At this point, you may be wondering, "How do you do that?" Well, you have just experienced many stories about other believers' Journey with Jesus; and though each person's story is unique, you too have a Journey to start to have this same relationship with God to inspire and motivate your own life.

First, we have to recognize the problem. It's that our sin keeps us from having a relationship with God. If we fail to connect with God on this side of eternity, we will face eternity without Him. The Bible talks about a literal heaven and a literal hell. And that heaven isn't filled with perfect people. It's filled with forgiven people.

The solution: Jesus came to earth and then died to fix that broken relationship. Jesus is the one that wiped us clean of our sins so that we could have a relationship with God forever: "For Christ also suffered once for sins, the righteous for the unrighteous, that he might bring us to God" (1 Peter 3:18 ESV). No matter where you are or where you have been, because of Jesus, you can know where you're going. He died for the sins of the whole world. That means mine… and that means yours.

Though I've shared stories about the faithfulness and value that my church has brought to me throughout my life, this really isn't about going to church. It's about going to the one who can save and heal you. His name is Jesus. Based on biblical scripture, it's the only name that matters. And the Bible makes this clear: "For 'everyone who calls on the name of the Lord will be saved'" (Romans 10:13 ESV). Not only did Jesus die to forgive you of your sins, but in rising from the grave, He gives you the opportunity for NEW LIFE.

In John 11:25 (ESV), Jesus said, "I am the resurrection and the life. Whoever believes in me, though he die, yet shall he live." And if you accept Jesus's death, burial and resurrection, you're no longer bound to the shackles of that old life; "therefore, if anyone is in Christ, he is a new creation. The old has passed away; behold, the new has come" (2 Corinthians 5:17 ESV).

As I shared throughout this book, PLEASE KNOW that starting your Journey with Jesus has nothing to do with how good you are and what you've done but how perfect He is and how He can help you.

> For by GRACE you have been saved
> through FAITH. And this is not your own doing;

it is the gift of God, not a result of works, so that no one may boast. (Ephesians 2:8–9 ESV; emphasis added)

So why not start your Journey today? What's stopping you?

If God is moving in your heart, pray this prayer to accept the gift of Jesus. It's not the prayer that does anything for you, but it helps you accept the gift of Jesus dying on the cross and the work that God is doing in your heart right now.

PRAY WITH ME: My Heavenly Father, thank you for sending Jesus to die for my sins. I accept that Jesus died in my place and forgave me. And I believe that Jesus rose again from the grave. I turn my life to You, and I turn from my old way of thinking about You. Take my life and give me a new one with You at the center. Amen.

CONGRATULATIONS! You have just taken the biggest step of faith in your life. If you are just starting your Journey with Jesus or renewing it, start talking to Him directly every day, throughout your day, or whenever. That's the most important message because He loves you, and He hears you!

Get connected. If you don't already have one, find a Christian friend or a church that teaches the Bible or a place where you can get support in this amazingly life-changing decision. This will help you grow and meet other people who are experiencing the beauty of the Journey with Jesus too!

> For God so loved the world, that he gave his only Son, that whoever believes in him should not perish but have eternal life. (John 3:16)

Close = Praise and Inspiration

✦

I received a gift from one of my employees early in my tenure at GOJO. It was a cute little book that was filled with encouraging words and vibrant pictures. I appreciated the gift and kept it in my office desk. As time would have it, the book got buried with all my other work stuff, and I had not seen or read it since years earlier when it was received. As my recent position was recently downsized, I had already boxed up my personal belongings months prior since the workplace changes required us to WFH, and there was no longer a need to have them at the office.

The few boxes that I had were now being stored in my home, and I wanted to clean them out to get rid of the old and start anew, so I began go through each box, looking at each item and assessing its value. When I got to the last box a couple days later, I found a TRUE GIFT. It was the little book titled *I Believe in You* by Sandy Gingras. There are only about forty pages in this tiny little book, but each page has an encouraging message and coordinated hand-drawn picture. When I got close to the end, I saw a message to amazingly assist in my inspiration, motivation, and encouragement to complete this work. It stated, "I believe in trusting the Journey, not the road's end." This was so significant for me, especially at this time. I feel strongly that God led me back to this book to encourage me and reinforce that it was time to share this book to encourage others. I have always referred to this work with the Journey suggestion, and I had also thought that when the book was completed, God would no longer have a reason for me… Boy, was that thinking wrong. Now I know that this is just the beginning of a new Journey for me to share and inspire us to live our best Journey. It excites me to enter into my future, thinking, *What's next?* **PRAISE REPORT!**

You never know when or where God has someone out there for you to help or for them to help you. Broaden your horizons, expand your bandwidth, and open your heart. Now watch God work in truly amazing ways. God uses the unexpected. We don't need to live holier than thou, or we wouldn't need Jesus. Remember, everyone has something to share, whether it be wisdom, experiences, friendship, prayer, food, time, a ride, and the like.

FREE WILL—it's your Journey; own it with the power of our Almighty God.

When I was raising my kids, I had a negative take on Halloween for what I believed was tied to its origins. The church we attended did not celebrate it either; they had a different take and alternately celebrated that time of year differently as a harvest-type festival. This was literally a party at the church, in a controlled environment, not door-to-door as the current tradition plays out. And as an FYI, if you google the origin of Halloween, you will find many different assumptions and stories. That is why I did not allow my children to go door-to-door on that celebrated evening of October 31.

Instead, I dressed them up at any given time throughout the year. I remember having so much fun dressing them up in homemade costumes when I took them out to the grocery store as mentioned earlier in this book. Let me tell you, it was a real attention-getter, and my kids had a blast. They never felt like they missed anything. But as they got older and my relationship with God became closer, my take on Halloween has been slightly altered, and although I love the harvest party and fellowship with other Christians, I look for positive ways to be more engaged with my community. By taking the time to hand out small tokens of appreciation for our youth in the neighborhood and be a friendly neighbor so others are open to my testimony when the door opens to share it. Let's face it, the kids are just internalizing you're not being home or not sharing as being "not a nice person." I use this example to share that even the things that are possibly meant for evil in this world can be used by God for good.

Years back, when I was volunteering at Gilda's Club, I was selected for an article for their monthly newsletter. They regularly selected volunteers to tell their story as to why they volunteer and what motivates them. My motivation was my brain tumor experience, and this was an amazing opportunity for me to give back. Well, that was my motivation, but throughout my five-year experience volunteering at Gilda's Club, I learned that God was using this opportunity for me to also learn and to be inspired as well.

There was a young lady whom I worked with often there named Lizzie. She was a cancer survivor. She taught me more about God's love and finding the joy in the Journey just by her positive attitude. I can't image how hard it was for her to demonstrate her positivity while going through extensive treatments throughout her young life, but she was a ray of sunshine and truly loved the Lord. I volunteered to give, but I most certainly received! **PRAISE REPORT!**

Similar to this story, have you ever had an experience that literally stuck with you for your entire life in an inspirational way? I have to share this story about true appreciation. When I was sixteen, I held my first real paid job working an entry-level position as a patient tray girl (meal delivery person) at a local hospital. I was making minimum wage ($3.35/hour), and I was grateful to have a job. I still have memories and sometimes dreams about the comradery shared between me and my coworkers there.

Well, mostly comradery, sometimes not always seeing eye to eye, but that's just life. This story is about the impact that I experienced when minimum wage was increased dramatically and went up to $5.42 while I was working in that position. WOW, I thought I was rich, and I was—rich in appreciation to God that my work valuation was respected by this increase. It impacted me so tremendously that I still hold that number as special in my heart and know that God was taking care of me even when I was not living a day-to-day personal relationship with Jesus. But my appreciation was in knowing that it was completely out of my control; it propelled me to work better and harder to earn that respect—an amazing lesson for a sixteen-year-old. It stuck throughout my career, and I work hard even today, knowing

God is my provider. I work to please Him by being the best I can be.
PRAISE REPORT!

As my life progressed, I worked in a sales capacity early in my professional career, and that experience taught me a great deal. It was with Mary Kay cosmetics and lasted for only a few years, but I learned so much.

First off, Mary Kay herself built her 2.5-billion-dollar global empire out of a small five-thousand-dollar investment because she was treated poorly by her previous employers. That's truly inspirational from a business and professional perspective, but even more impressive and inspiring are the Christian principles she kept at utmost importance to lead her business. Her motto was "God first, family second, job third." A couple of her most inspirational quotes include: "God didn't have time to make a nobody, only a somebody" and "I believe that each of us has God-given talents waiting to be brought to fruition." She truly believed this way, and it was emulated throughout my experience with the company. Thank you, Mary Kay, for being an upright role model for all businesswomen and allowing Jesus to lead you in all areas of your amazing life. And although you are enjoying paradise, your legacy on earth lives on!

As a contribution to my legacy, I wanted to share the following top ten "*Wendyisms*" as we refer to them in our family. Some of these I have adopted from amazing role models in my life and others I created myself, and they are significant in my life's Journey. I hope you can appreciate them, and feel free to adopt in your life the ones that touch your heart specifically as well.

1. We are God's heart beating in our own communities.
2. Work like it is in your hands; pray as if it is in God's. (Thanks, Mike!)
3. Make decisions with the best information you have at the time. No regrets. (Thanks, Mom!)
4. "Without vision my people will perish" (Proverbs 29:18). Pray for vision and be specific in your prayer. Let God be the author of the desires of your heart and you will not only be filled with love; you will exude it.

5. Get up, dress up, show up, and *never give up*! (Thanks, Sue!)
6. Collaborative engagement equals success.
7. Learn something new every day.
8. If you let something, some thought or a desire, consume you, it's not from God. Let God consume you and His will, will be perfected through you! (Thanks, Benjamin Franklin!)
9. "Promise me you'll always REMEMBER: You're braver that you believe, stronger than you seem, and smarter than you think." (Thanks, Christopher Robin!)
10. You never look good trying to make someone else look bad.

As I have shared many stories of others who are so thankful and feel remarkably blessed to be on this Journey with Jesus, what we have collectively learned is that God's way of working in our lives typically involves others acting in obedience and God speaking to their hearts.

Seven years ago, Debbie had such a bad day that she angrily sat down and told God that if He seriously cared about her, He would send someone to be with her, and immediately the door began to knock. There stood her friend, and she said, "God sent me to come see you as I was trying to finish my housework. I just had to stop and listen." It's true that God doesn't always answer our prayers that quickly or intensely, but these things DO happen on a daily, weekly, monthly, and even yearly basis. Almost expect it, my friend! Always be thankful and grateful and recognize that God's answers aren't always what we think they might be, but they are the BEST thing for us personally. Hopefully, you have been inspired to be OPEN to that.

This reminds me of a very notable author and public inspirational speaker named Joni Eareckson Tada. She talks about her life and what happened to her as a teenager, when only months after praying for a closer relationship with God, she had a very traumatic accident that could have shortened her life altogether, but instead, she became a paraplegic. And despite praying for a healing from this condition resulting from a poor decision in her life, God allowed it to remain. And after a great deal of hopelessness, pain, and overall brokenness, she became open to God in her weakness…and how amazing her life became. **PRAISE REPORT!** Look her up. She has a truly amazing story of her Journey. One thing she quoted that I will never forget and really shows her gratefulness to God is the following as I paraphrase: I would rather be in this wheelchair, knowing God, than to be on my feet not knowing Him. (Thank you, Joni!)

Overall, during this most interesting and amazing Journey of preparing this book and meeting with other women (and a few gentlemen) who love the Lord, I have been encouraged by these interviews. I can see clearly how a positive mindset is helpful and uplifting to those in the midst of their own storms. There always seems to be a healing in the process as well. **PRAISE REPORT!**

As part of this inspiration-provoking close, please see my top seven interview takeaways:

1. Give of your time and talent.
2. Focus on what you *can* do, as opposed to what you can't. What do you focus on? The truth is that we can't always change what is going on around us, but we can control and change our focus. You may have heard the saying that idle hands promote the playground of sin. Have focus, and when you can't find it, pray for vision!
3. Turn from sin, or it will destroy you. Yes, it's a true blessing that God forgives us of our confessed sin, but we still have to face the consequences.
4. God abundantly provides.
5. God is our counselor. Read John 14:1—a message of hope to not let your heart be troubled.
6. Just because something on the surface appears to be "good" doesn't necessarily mean it is for you. Learn to consult with God first and trust His inspired direction, otherwise referred to as the Holy Spirit's leading.
7. Mindset—keep it on Jesus. Whatever you set your mind on will be what you see in any given situation (back to the car or color example).

By putting Jesus on the top of your mind daily, you will have a better time recognizing His work in your life throughout the day. It's like He reaches down and directly interferes in your life. This is where trust comes into play.

Proverbs 3:5–6 tells us that we are to trust the Lord with all of our hearts and lean not on our own understanding, to acknowledge Him in all our ways and He will make our paths straight. I just love the sound of that passage, but have you ever thought that to have trust, you must first realize there must be unanswered questions? (Thank you, Joyce!) If we knew everything, we would not need to trust.

Only God can foresee our future because He has ordained it. Who else's hand would you rather place your trust in, man or God? Even though we can read the stories of others who have placed their trust in God and experienced God's faithfulness, we must all learn for ourselves that He is faithful and trustworthy in OUR lives. The only way you can truly experience this is by stepping out in faith when He is leading you to do amazingly wonderful things. As you move forward and see how He is guiding you and supporting those steps, that trust begins to grow. This is how your relationship gets stronger roots.

Thank you for taking time to experience the details of the tapestry of thread throughout my life and of many others to demonstrate God's protection and provision in times when we can't even see them. My prayer is that you are encouraged and inspired by the sharing of these many illustrations of how God *can* and *will* provide light in a time of trouble to bring hopefulness, if we only ask, trust, and stay open to His grace. Build your relationship with God today and let your Journey begin!

Please contact me if you have been inspired and have a story of your own that you want to be shared. I can be reached at rocco1411@verizon.net.

I am available for public speaking events to encourage, inspire, motivate, and share the message of fostering a personal day-to-day relationship with God.

Wendy Gill Rocco

The Lord bless you, and keep you: The Lord make his face shine upon you, and be gracious unto you: The Lord lift up his countenance upon you, and give you peace. (Numbers 6:24–26)

About the Author

✦

This book is about enjoying and appreciating every day of your life even in seemingly bad times or through instances of bad experiences. To provide insight about the author, please know that I am a regular person, with issues, problems, and shortcomings as we all do. Let's face it, and please don't be fooled—NOBODY is perfect.

In my world, this book is twenty-plus years in the making and is most definitely a vision given to me from God. You might ask, so after that long, what has gotten me to this point to completion? My response is I am leaning on the Bible verse that states, "He who began a good work in you will be faithful to complete it" (Phil 1:6), and He most certainly created a path and the timing for His glory, as since my original vision, He has allowed me to experience many unexpected life challenges to share with you that demonstrate His mercy and faithfulness.

Thank you for taking time to experience the details of God's tapestry throughout my life and of so many others to demonstrate God's influence, protection, and provision in hard times even when we can't see it through the process. My prayer is that you are encouraged and inspired by our sharing of how God can and will provide light in a time of trouble to bring hopefulness, if we only ask, trust, and stay open to His grace.

Please feel free to contact me if you have been inspired and have a "Journey" of your own that you would like to be considered for print because this is just the first of many more *JWJ* inspiration to be shared. I can be reached at rocco1411@verizon.net and am available for public speaking events to encourage, inspire, motivate, and share the message of fostering a personal day-to-day relationship with Jesus.

Wendy Gill Rocco

The Lord bless you and keep you: The Lord make his face shine upon you and be gracious unto you: The Lord lift up his countenance upon you and give you peace. (Numbers 6:24–26)

CPSIA information can be obtained
at www.ICGtesting.com
Printed in the USA
LVHW011122040623
748794LV00034B/218

9 798887 519326